The Carthage Option

J.C. PACHECO

To my Mother, 'S', Wendy, Sunny, and Stella

CONTENTS

THE SERIES...so far...

The Inseparable Gang of Happy Girls

Ptolemaic England

The Ghosts of Manchukuo

The Last Emperor of the City

The Carthage Option

1 LITTLE RHODESIA

Gemma—The Carthage Option—The Chaos Bracelet

LONDON

December 2019

Gemma sat at the large wooden table in her tiny studio flat. The wooden table also doubled as her desk. Outside the sky was blue, the air crisp, and a wind from the north had brought with it colder than normal winter temperatures. It was forecast to snow the next day, but looking at the clear blue skies, one would never guess it.

Gemma opened the purple box that she had placed on the table a moment before. Inside was a bracelet of 18 carat white gold set with a variety of precious gems. It was beautiful. Grey had bought it for her. She had been forced to accept it from two of his minions on the dark street in front of her apartment building in London. Just outside on the street below, almost a year ago, a man had stopped her and offered her the white gold bracelet—a gift from Grey. She had been forced to accept it. The event would prove to be pivotal. It was the night that Gemma had told Poppy about Grey's relentlessness. And it was two weeks later that Gemma would finally confide in Poppy and tell her what Grey had done to her that night in Primrose Hill.

Gemma had kept the bracelet in a drawer ever since. Now, almost a year to the day later, Gemma held it in her hands. What did it represent to her? Grey? The trauma she had suffered? Gemma had thought about this for a long time.

1

No. The bracelet now represented the bond between two inseparable friends. Gemma, with the help of friends, had survived. Grey had not. Nor had the people that had stopped her that night on the street. They were no longer alive. Gemma was.

Gemma slid the bracelet onto her wrist. She looked at it. Yes, the bracelet meant a lot to her. The Chaos bracelet represented Poppy's love and devotion to her. Gemma would add this bracelet to her jewelry box. She would wear it often. Gemma had grown tired of lowering her gaze and avoiding the stares of her enemies. Gemma had done nothing wrong. She had been wronged. Yes, the 4th Baron was right. From now on, Gemma would hold her head up high. *Let her enemies turn away and avert their gaze*. It no longer mattered to her. **Gemma was now free.** Poppy and Winter had freed her. God had freed her. Gemma had not given up; God had not given up on Gemma.

Gemma exhaled.

Gemma was now free.

Gemma—The Carthage Option—The Ruins

MIDLANDS-HASEGAWA UNIVERSITY

It was the cold of a wintery day at the beginning of December that had awoken Wren. Wren pulled the white duvet up over her shoulders in an attempt to stay warm. It didn't work. She opened her eyes and looked around the room. Only bare white walls and a white sash window. Outside it was overcast and grey natural light filled the room. It was freezing.

Wren, in dark blue pyjamas (with white piping), sat up and bed and looked around. What time was it? She got out of bed and put on her white slippers. She stood up. It was as if she were standing outside. Wren took a few steps and grabbed the tartan flannel robe off of a wooden peg. She put it on and tied it. She was still freezing cold. Wren picked up her quartz wristwatch and checked the time: 7:53am.

There was a light knock at her door.

Wren walked over and opened the glossy white door to her dorm room. Standing in the doorway was the flaxen haired Freya. Freya, in a pair of pale blue pyjama bottoms, a pair of white slippers, a blue quilted jacket, and her red, blue, and purple All Saints scarf, was standing in the doorway.

'The heat is out,' said Freya through chattering teeth. Wren could see two raven-haired Asian students, both in thin padded jackets and pyjamas walking down the hallway behind Freya through the winter morning gloom. Freya smiled. 'The entire hall is without heat. May I come in?'

'Yes, please, come in.'

Freya entered Wren's room and closed the door. Freya, a natural beauty, gilded effortlessly into the small dorm room. Freya moved with the grace and manner of the noble born. Freya, like Wren, was from an ancient noble family. Wren and Freya both moved and behaved unconsciously in the same manner.

'Some of the students have electric blankets and room heaters. I found a group of Taiwanese girls gathering in a room down the hall. They are all in pyjamas and winter coats and sitting around a room heater. Suga is lucky. She has a room with a fireplace. She invited me to come to her room. She said you are welcome to come with me,' said Freya as she stood with her arms crossed trying to warm herself.

'This is what it is like at my house in the winter,' said Wren. 'The heat is always going out. The bedrooms all have fireplaces; that's how we stay warm. The Jacobean fireplace in my room is made of marble. I am use to this. I have an electric blanket. You can borrow it. I also have three wool blankets from home. I will use them,' said Wren and she smiled.

'Thank you, Wren. I'm ill-prepared for everything. At All Saints, things like this never happened. I guess Muddy Hills will be an adventure.'

'Yes, like army training.'

'Yes, you're right,' said Freya happily. 'This will toughen us up.'

There was a knock on the door. Wren opened it. It was Suga, the Scottish undergraduate, stage actress, and resident seductress. The curvy and blonde Suga, in pale blue pyjama bottoms, blue velvet slippers, and a heavy knit beige jumper, entered.

'Suga', short for 'Sugar', was beautiful. The only daughter of a Scottish farmer and former Para, 'Suga' was an aspiring actress and heartbreaker. Wren had seen her in the residence hall (how could she miss her?) on an almost daily basis, but had only spoken to her once. She found Ava (Suga's real name) to be rather sweet. Suga was friends with (The Honourable) Wallis, who lived upstairs from her in an alcove with three Japanese undergraduates.

'My room is warm and we are baking potatoes in the fireplace right now. Would you like to join us?' asked Suga in a gentle Scottish lilt.

'Thank you, Suga,' said Wren. 'I haven't had breakfast yet. We bake potatoes in our kitchen at home all the time.'

'Thank you, Suga, I would like to bake a potato too,' said Freya.

Suga smiled. 'Wallis is there with her roommates. So is Pasha. You'll like her, Wren. She is Laotian.'

THE FIREPLACE
Freya knocked gently on the glossy white door and the diminutive 'Pasha' answered. Pasha (her real name was Pashay) was a Laotian undergraduate. She was also acting in the play with Freya. So was Suga; she was one of Cleopatra's slaves…

Pasha was wearing navy blue pyjamas and a beige cricket sweater that looked to be three sizes too big for her. Pasha was tiny, delicate, and attractive. Her glossy black hair was tied back with a white ribbon. Pasha flashed a white smile. 'I'm so happy you could join us, Freya,' said Pashay in her accented English.

'Thank you for inviting us,' replied Freya. 'Pasha, I would like to introduce you to my friend Wren,' said Freya.

'Pasha smiled and said, 'It's nice to meet you, Wren.'

Wren smiled and said, 'It's nice to meet you, too, Pasha.'

The girls entered the large white walled room. At one end of the room was a marble fireplace. The fire within it crackled with warmth.

There were also four white sash windows and two beds: one covered with a white cotton duvet, the other with several layers of wool blankets (in tartan colors). There were two wooden desks and in the center of the room was a wooden table. This room had once been set aside for the wealthier students. Now the room belonged to whoever was fortunate enough to be assigned it.

Suga's side of the room was quite cozy. A wool tartan cape hung from a wooden peg next to her bed. There were three large white pillows on her bed. The wool blankets covered white Egyptian cotton sheets. Suga's bed was unmade. On Suga's desk there were several textbooks, a silver pen, several mechanical pencils, a yellow highlighter, and several notebooks. There was also a white ceramic mug. A blue quilted jacket hung from a wooden peg above her bed.

Pasha's side of the room was in military order. Pasha's narrow bed was carefully made and resembled a bed found in a five star hotel. Her desk was bare. Her textbooks sat on a small shelf next to the desk. Pasha's half of the room looked almost clinical.

Wallis, the future 12th Baroness, and her three Japanese roommates (all clad in thin padded jackets) were gathered around the fireplace trying to stay warm. Wallis, blonde and blue eyed, was wearing a heavy knit beige sweater with a pair of pale blue cotton pyjamas and white slippers. She was holding a white ceramic plate in her hands with a tinfoil wrapped baked potato inside. Steam rose off of the tin foiled spud. Wallis smiled.

'Good morning. Yes, your eyes doth not deceive you. We are baking potatoes in the oak ash and embers in the fireplace. There is butter and pepper on the table,' said Wallis in her posh intonation. Wallis's blonde hair, the color of straw, was piled onto her head and held up with silver hairpins.

Freya noticed a white ceramic bowl on the table with several bluish purple potatoes inside. They had been washed earlier and were still wet. Next to the ceramic bowl was a boxed roll of tin foil and several white ceramic plates and some inexpensive silverware.

'The potatoes came from my family farm. The potatoes are Arran Victories. I've always really liked the bluish purple color of them. Please, have one and join us,' said Suga.

Freya smiled and said, 'Thank you, Suga.'

Wren also thanked Suga as she took one of the bluish purple Arran Victories from the white bowl. Wren took a metal fork and stabbed the potato several times. After she had added a dash of butter she carefully and expertly wrapped it in tinfoil. She then walked over to the fireplace and using a set of iron fireplace tongs, carefully laid it in the glowing orange embers of the fireplace next to several others.

There were three wooden chairs around the fireplace, each used by the undergraduates in turns as they monitored the progress of their potatoes.

'The fireplace really warms the room well,' said Kokoro. She was one of Wallis's alcove gang. She was playing a Roman soldier in the play. Kokoro was very sweet and often unintentionally funny as she spoke of things in her deadpan English.

'This is how we usually heat the house,' said Wren. 'The furnace is always going out. It was installed in the 1930s. It works well, when it works.'

THE ENGLISH CIVIL WAR
'Wren lives in a castle,' said Wallis. 'Castles are notoriously drafty.'

'It's more of a fortified manor house. The family castle is a few miles away. No one has lived in the castle since the English Civil War. The Roundheads destroyed it. It's *rather* too sad.'

'Why didn't your family rebuild it?' asked Pasha.

'We were Royalist exiles on the continent for over a decade. We returned with the Restoration. The family only had enough money to rebuild the manor house. The castle has been a ruin ever since.'

'That's so sad,' said Pasha. 'Your poor parents. How heartbreaking.'

'Yes, the whole family is heartbroken over it.'

'When did this happen?' asked Pasha.

'In 1649,' said Wren sadly.

'What?' replied Pasha.

THE ROYALISTS
'It might as well have been yesterday, Pasha,' said Wren gloomily.

'Yes, you are right, Wren. The Parliamentarians were awful. Our family castle was leveled during the English Civil War too. It's only a pile of stones now. We used some of them to build our new house in 1789. The year the French Revolution began,' said Wallis.

'I understand,' said Masako. Masako was a rather tall Japanese undergraduate. She was very pale and slender. While rather plain looking, Masako was elegant in manner and spoke English perfectly. She was also picking up Wallis's Sloaney intonation. 'My family's castle was destroyed in the 1400s and it still hurts. My ancestors were Daimyō. The loss of our lands and castle remain a deep wound.'

The village still celebrates Oak Apple Day on the Nine and Twentieth Day of May,' said Wren. 'On Oak Apple Day everyone marches through the village holding flower and oak leaf decorated sticks, whilst following a Royalist battle flag and the village brass band. The march goes first to the medieval church for an Anglican service, and then to houses in the village who host refreshments. My family still has the original Royalists flags carried into battle by our ancestors. We don't fly them anymore; they are too fragile. The family had copies made in 1910. We use them. My father, the 23rd Baron, leads the event every year. It's really interesting. Quite solemn at the beginning, but then happy when we commemorate the Restoration of the King,' said Wren reflectively. 'The church bells ring joyously at the end of the church service.'

'I would like to go with you one year, Wren, said Wallis.

'Me, too,' said Pasha happily.

'Yes, I would like to attend too,' said Freya.

Wren smiled.

A LETTER FROM MERCIA
December 1, 2019

Dear Wren,

I hope you are having a good time at Muddy Hills. Have you made any new friends there? Please feel free to invite them to the house.

Your father has had the roof properly repaired. We had to sell one of the lorries to afford it. Can you believe it? The old Thornycroft hadn't run in decades. It had just sat in the coach house gathering dust. A man knocked on the door last October, and we sold it to him for a small fortune. Everything about the lorry was original. That had been very important to him. Well, we didn't want it. We couldn't give it away for decades. No one wanted it. Well, long story short, Wren, we had the money to repair the roof. We wanted to surprise you. The roof looks glorious now and there no leaks.

We had the roof repaired three weeks ago while you were visiting Portugal. How is my sister? She always tells me how happy she is living in Portugal. She says Portugal reminds her of Rhodesia. Did you go riding?

We have also repainted all of the rooms, including the servants' quarters. We used a hundred gallons of white paint.

We didn't have enough money to bring in electricians to fix the electrical works in the house. It will be so nice to have electricity in every room of the house one day. How wonderful it will be to walk through the house at night without tripping over something or banging into a wall. For now, we still carry torches with us at night.

We still don't have enough money to repair the tiles in the entry hall, but we will repair them eventually. The furnace is next on the list. However, the plumbing has been restored in all of the rooms. Wren, the house feels brand new. I know there is still a lot of work to do, Wren, but we have made progress.

Please take the train home one weekend and see for yourself. Please do feel free to invite your friends from Midlands-Hasegawa. I hope you are making good friends there. Don't worry, the house, while still a work in progress, is looking much better. Yes, most of the house is empty, but we will need the extra space for when the ghosts return.

We have always been proud of you, Wren. Please take good care of yourself. Are you taking your vitamins? Do you still exercise every day? Please remember to get plenty of sleep. That's important.

Love,

Mummy

P.S. The Thornycroft is destined for a museum in Manchester. How wonderful.

THE DINING HALL

The dining hall was heated. Never had heat been so appreciated by so many. Most of the students kept their jackets on while they had lunch. Lunch today was especially good: Melton Mowbray pork pies and Coventry Godcake. There was also a good selection of steamed vegetables. The frozen undergraduates of ~~Rhodes~~ Midlands-Hasegawa were grateful for the hot food.

Also, the mysterious and largely forgotten Coventry Godcake was delicious. The three sided cake had three slashes across it; 'the threes' represented the Holy Trinity. Coventry Godcake was not unknown to Freya. She had received one every year since her 4th birthday from her godmother Gemma. Gemma always baked the cake herself. Freya ate it slowly, savoring every bite. The cake made Freya happy. It reminded her of her Godmother. The cold discomfort of the day melted away with every bite. Yes, the furnace would be repaired—eventually. But that was a relative small matter. What mattered were the people you loved. Freya, surrounded by the undergraduates of Midlands-Hasegawa, was happy.

Wren, her newest friend, sat across from her. Wallis, Pasha, and Suga were seated on either side of her. Wallis, her tortoise shell sunglasses tilted back on her head, looked like a movie star from the 1950s. She had unbuttoned her dark blue frock coat (with silver buttons) and happily consumed Coventry Godcake.

'When will Jinx be back?' asked Suga.

'Tomorrow. I hope. She should be crossing the Atlantic at this moment. I haven't heard a word from her since she left,' said Freya.

'She'll probably be exhausted. I can't even begin to imagine what it must be like to fly four days out nine,' said Wallis. 'My parents once flew on the Concorde to London from New York. They said it was a lot of fun.'

'My father used to jump out of planes, not fly in them. He says that's much more enjoyable,' said the flaxen haired Suga happily.

'Jump out? Was your father a soldier?' asked Wallis.

'Yes, my father was a Para,' said Suga and she smiled.

'My father was in the Welsh Guards,' said Wallis. 'Was your father in the army, Freya?'

'No. But my grandfather was. He was a Para.'

Suddenly a tiny hand bell rang. The students looked towards the end of the cavernous dining hall. An elderly university administrator, in dark coat and striped regimental tie, stood behind the wooden podium, a large painting of Cecil Rhodes behind him. A hushed silence filled the hall. The aged, thin, white-haired Rhodesian began to speak.

'The university apologizes for the heating problem in the residence halls. The repairmen are now working on the furnaces and we hope to have the heating system repaired within the next four or five days.'

A loud murmur moved through the dining hall. Some of the students had gasped at the announcement.

'Extra blankets will be given out to each of you this afternoon. Also, we have purchased three dozen room heaters from the local stores. They were all that were available. Please consider sharing rooms for the next couple of days. The room heaters are quite effective. Thank you.'

The elderly Rhodesian stepped away from the podium and made his way back to his table. A low murmur filled the hall.

'You can stay with me,' said Suga. Yes, my room is large enough. I'll help you carry your mattresses down the hall.'

'Thank you, Suga, but we have two room heaters in the alcove. We will be warm enough, said Wallis.

'I'll see you tonight then,' said Freya.

'*Rather,*' said Wren happily. It's freezing in my room. I have an electric blanket I can bring too.'

'I like cold weather,' said the tiny Pasha. It's a nice change from the tropical heat of Laos.

THE GIRLS' RESIDENCE HALL

That afternoon, a brand new Japanese SUV pulled up to the hall filled with cardboard boxes. The boxes were placed on a large wooden table in the entry hall. Three undergraduates, members of the university's rowing club, handed a blanket to each student as she entered the hall.

The drab surplus army blankets smelled of mothballs.

Freya and Wren carried their wool blankets to Suga's room together.

'You know, I don't think these blankets have been issued since the Boer War,' said Wren as she examined her wool blanket.

Freya smiled. 'Probably not.'

EVENING IN THE RESIDENCE HALL

Freya and Wren had placed their mattresses in front of the marble fireplace. Two electric room heaters, glowing brightly and radiating heat, had been placed between Suga and Pasha's beds at the other end of the room.

Suga studied quietly at her desk. Pasha was still out somewhere—probably studying in the (heated) library. The only sounds in the room were the crackling of the fire, the sound of metal expanding and contracting which came from the room heaters, and the ticking of a clock on the mantelpiece. Occasionally the wind would rattle the windows.

Freya, lying in her bed a few feet away from the fireplace, was studying her history notes. Wren was reading a book on the Boer War. Dinner had been good: steak. And yes, steak also reminded Freya of her Godmother and made her feel happy. It was time to write Gemma a letter.

A LETTER FROM THE MIDLANDS

December 5, 2019

Dear Godmother,

The first rehearsal of The Ptolemies went extremely well. I felt as if I had been transported back in time. I can't wait for you to see the play. I am nervous, but I'm also excited. Since you played Cleopatra at Oxford and Mummy played Cleopatra at All Saints, I am following in the steps of those I love.

Jinx should return tomorrow. I haven't heard anything from her. I suppose she has been overwhelmed by it all. It will be nice to have her back. I have missed her. I'm looking forward to hearing her stories.

I have also made new friends through a Hon who lives at the end of the hall. Her name is Wren, and she is from an ancient noble family in northwest England. She is terribly nice. One day I will introduce her to you. Her mother is Rhodesian. Wren spent half of November in Portugal on her aunt's cattle ranch. Wren loves riding and hunting. Mummy will love her.

I am relieved that Poppy is back at home with the twins. Mummy told me over the phone that twins are adorable. Waverly. What a nice name for Poppy's daughter. Yes, Waverly—a meadow of quivering aspens. What a beautiful name. Waverly. Yes. I really love it. And Poppy has named her son Arthur. How nice. And as godmother to Arthur, Gemma, I know you will do everything to make his life even happier—if that is possible. Yes, Waverly and Arthur are beautiful and sweet additions to the family. Mummy and Daddy are excited about being a godparents to little Waverly. Sharing the responsibility with Külli will be a lot of fun. Little Arthur and Waverly will no doubt be frequent guests in Marble Arch.

Louise and Aurelia have both applied to Muddy Hills. I am sure they will be accepted. At least I hope so. I hope to share an alcove room with them and Jinx.

Today they served Coventry Godcake in the dining hall. It was heavenly. Of course, I thought of you, Godmother.

Love,

Freya

Gemma—The Carthage Option—Rex

THE MIDLANDS

Rex was freezing. Yes, the furnace had gone out, not in one, but both
residence halls. How was that possible? Well, both furnaces were
connected, somehow. And all of the giant furnaces at ~~Rhodes~~ Midlands–
Hasegawa University had been installed in the 1920s.

Rex and his Taiwanese roommate Albert were fortunate: There room had a
small fireplace. And fortunately for them, a chimney sweep had cleaned all
of the chimneys at the university last summer, so they could use it.

Rex and Albert had spent the afternoon walking into town and buying
firewood from a local. They had carried it back to school in a borrowed
wheel barrow. They had made several trips up and down the stairs carrying
the firewood. Yes, the afternoon had been a tough one.

Neither Rex nor Albert really knew how to start a fire. It looked easy in
movies. Not so much in real life. Rex had telephoned Bramwell. Rex didn't
know Bram that well, but he knew that Bram was the son of a farmer,
surely he would know. He did. 'Bram' arrived a few minutes later and
started the fire quite easily.

Rex and Albert invited Bram to stay with them in their room that night.
After all, they had one of the larger rooms and Bram could sleep in the
main room with them. Rex and Albert were going to move there mattresses
out of the bedroom and into the sitting room.

'Yes, thank you. This room is much warmer than the three wool blankets I
am sleeping under now,' replied Bramwell happily.

The blond Bramwell smiled. Bram, shy and quiet, didn't have any friends at
Muddy Hills. That appeared to have changed.

'I am also a good cook. I have a cast iron pan in my room. Let's see what
we can cook up this weekend,' said Bram happily.

Gemma—The Carthage Option—The Return

MIDLANDS-HASEGAWA UNIVERSITY

The dark blue taxi cab came to a complete stop at the edge of the leaf covered grass quad. It was night and very dark. The stone Victorian residence halls were black hulks outlined by the illumination from the lights of the empty plinth in the middle of the quad and the lamps which lit up the ornate stone entrances to the halls. Jinx, in the backseat of the taxi, noticed something immediately: Only about a third of the dormitory windows had lights on in their rooms. This was all highly unusual. Had something befallen the students while Jinx was away? Had the Black Death returned to Muddy Hills? Had there been mass arrests of the politically incorrect at the university? (No, that couldn't be it, there wouldn't be any lights on in the halls had that been the case.)

Jinx thanked the taxi driver who had picked her up at the train station and climbed out of the dark blue car with her leather box suitcase, blue canvas overnight bag, and a large paper shopping bag from a store in Kyoto. A box would be arriving at the university post office from Tokyo in a day or two.

A blast of cold air struck Jinx as soon as she stepped out of the taxi. She adjusted her wool scarf.

The Goddess of Ginza had returned. Jinx's glossy black hair had been cut into a chin length bob a few hours before the fashion show in Tokyo the week before; now Jinx truly was The Girl in the Black Helmet. Jinx's complexion was clear and translucent. Jinx had discovered a lot about herself in the last three weeks. She had recognized how beautiful she really was. She had seen what others had been seeing for so long. The beauty which gazed back at her from the mirror no longer belonged to a stranger. For every change in her; however, there was something that had remained unchanged. Jinx could sense that the most fragile pieces of her had remained as fragile as ever. Jinx hoped that she would find success; not for herself, but for her family. Jinx wanted to provide for what remained of her family. They had been uprooted and exiled. Her parents and grandparents were tired. They just wanted to rest. Jinx would help them. For the first time in Jinx's life, she had the financial means to help them. She would.

Clad in a pair of blue wool trousers, a white cotton blouse, and a blue blazer, Jinx made her way towards the girls' residence hall. It was freezing cold; Jinx could see her breath in the cold night air. No one was outside. Jinx checked her quartz wristwatch: 8:45pm.

Jinx was a little worried. Had something happened? If so, why hadn't she been contacted?

Jinx arrived at the front of the hall and slowly climbed the few stone steps up to the large wooden double doors carrying her luggage, her silky hair looked bluish black in the light given off by the lamps which adorned either side of the ornately carved stone entrance. Jinx was exhausted. The cold air had snapped her out of her drowsy state, but now, the exhaustion was returning. She just wanted to go to bed. Jinx entered the entry hall. It was fully lit. There were three cardboard boxes on the wooden table in the middle of the lobby. Several folded wool blankets sat next to the boxes. The entry hall smelled like mothballs. It was freezing inside the hall. No heat? There was no one around.

Jinx walked wearily down the hall until she reached the door to her room. She felt better already. Soon she would be reunited with Freya, give her her gift, and then go to sleep. Jinx noticed that no light was coming from underneath the door. The hallway was quiet. This was strange. Jinx felt like she was in a movie.

She unlocked the door and entered the dorm room. It was dark. She turned on the lights. Freya wasn't there. Her thin mattress, sheets, pillows, and blankets were gone. So were her books. Jinx put down her luggage and walked over to Freya's wardrobe. She opened the wooden door and looked inside. Most of Freya's clothes were gone. Gone. Had something happened? Had something terrible happened to Freya? Had she been injured in a car accident on the way back to Muddy Hills? Oh, she should have stayed, then Freya would not have driven so fast. Was this some kind of cosmic punishment for daring to fly too high? Had Jinx, like Icarus, fallen to the Earth? A sense of panic suddenly filled Jinx; tears welled up in her eyes. She turned around and scanned the room. No one was there.

Jinx walked over to her bed and sat down.

Be calm, Jinx. It's probably nothing. Don't panic. Why are panicking? Is it because you realize how important Freya is to you? No. You have always appreciated Freya. Freya was your dearest friend in the world.

Freya took out her smartphone; the battery was dead. Jinx put the phone in her coat pocket.

'Hello. Hi Jinx. Do you remember me? My name is Wren,' said the strikingly beautiful teenage girl standing in the doorway clad in a pair of dark blue pyjamas, a navy blue wool coat, and a pair of white slippers. The young woman's honey blonde hair was half way down her back and her honey blonde bangs partially obscured her blue eyes. The young, blonde, Rhodesian girl smiled.

Jinx had met Wren at a Rhodesia Club meeting in September and found her to be rude and arrogant. Jinx didn't like her. Rhodesian or not.

'Where is Freya?' asked Jinx quietly as she wiped the tears from her eyes.

'She's with us in Suga's room down the hall. Well, way down the hall; on the other side of the building. The furnace went out yesterday. Suga has a fireplace and two room heaters, so we moved in with her.

'What?'

'The furnace went out in the residence hall. Everyone is camping out in other rooms. It's quite fun, really.'

Jinx felt a huge wave of relief and a weight lifted off of her shoulders. Freya was alright. Jinx had another chance with her. The moment that she thought she had lost Freya had left her stomach in knots. It was a feeling she had only felt one other time: When her brother was murdered in a farm invasion in ~~Rhodesia~~ Zimbabwe.

Jinx was still sitting on her bed and looking at Wren when Freya, in a pair of navy blue pyjamas and a pale blue v-neck cashmere sweater, appeared next to her in the doorway. Freya's blonde hair was loose and rested on her shoulders. Freya flashed her white smile.

'Jinx! You're back. How was Tokyo?' asked Freya happily. And then Freya noticed that Jinx had been crying. She turned to Wren and said quietly, 'We'll come down to the room in a minute. I'm going to help Jinx with her mattress, alright?'

'Sure,' said Wren quietly. Wren quickly disappeared down the hallway.

Freya entered the room and quietly closed the glossy white door behind her. She walked over to Jinx and stood before her. 'May I sit down?'

'Yes.'

Freya sank down into the white duvet. Sitting next to Jinx, Freya asked, 'What's wrong, Jinx? Did something happen to you in Japan?'

Jinx started to choke back tears. 'I thought you were dead. I thought you had been killed in a traffic accident. Your bedding was gone, even your mattress. Your books, most of your clothes were missing. I thought I had lost you.'

Freya felt a jolt move through her. Jinx had had a bad shock. Freya hadn't anticipated this happening. She hadn't expected the heat to go out. She had expected that she would be studying at her desk when Jinx returned from Tokyo. So had Jinx. Freya had learned to be understanding from her Godmother.

'Oh, Jinx. I'm sorry. I really am. I should have emailed you and explained what was happening. I didn't want to bother you in Japan. I'm sorry.'

'All I could think of was when they murdered my brother. All of those emotions came flooding back to me. It's horrible, Freya. I miss my brother. He was always sweet and kind to me. He never raised his voice or had an unkind word for anyone. Why did they have to murder him? Is this the reward for being a good person?'

Freya felt absolutely horrible. A feeling filled her that she never had felt before. Though completely unintentional, she had hurt her friend Jinx. Yes, it was unintentional, but it had still hurt her. Jinx was fragile. Freya knew that.

'Jinx, I love you. I would never do anything to hurt you. I would…(No, don't say that. Jinx doesn't want to lose you, Freya.) I would never do anything to hurt you. I'm sorry.'

Jinx now had tears streaking down her face. She struggled to regain her composure. Freya put her arm around her and held one of Jinx's small, soft hands in hers.

'I have another chance with you, Freya. I don't have another with my brother. I'm glad you're alright. It would have destroyed me if something bad had happened to you.'

'Nothing will happen to me, Jinx. I'll always be here for you. I promise,' said Freya.

'I'm sorry, Freya. Sometimes I can't control my emotions. It's not your fault. You've done nothing wrong. My past keeps coming back to haunt me.'

'If you like we could stay here tonight. I could get a room heater from Suga and we could stay here in our room together,' said Freya. Jinx, at that moment, thought she could see Freya's breath materializing in the wintery cold of the unheated room.

Jinx smiled and then said, 'It's freezing, Freya. We would have to build a campfire to stay the night in here.'

'How about we take your bedding down to Suga's room? I could bake you a potato in her fireplace,' said Freya.

'Okay, yah!' said Jinx happily as she wiped away her tears.

Freya smiled and hugged Jinx tightly.

'Freya? Are you friends with Wren? I thought you didn't like her.'

'Oh, well, she's actually *rather* sweet. Her story is a bit complicated, but she is really a good person under all of her imperiousness. My mother used to be like Wren until earlier this year. That's a long story too. Please give Wren another chance. She is good-hearted. Really,' said Freya.

'Alright.'

Freya then noticed the raven-haired Jinx's hair had been cut into a razor sharp bob. 'Jinx. Your hair. I really like it.'

'It was for the fashion show. The designer wanted me to have this hairstyle. Did I look better with long hair?' asked Jinx while wiping away tears.

'I like it. Jinx, you are beautiful no matter how long or short your hair is,' said Freya.

'Thank you, Freya. I'm glad you like it. You always say nice things to me. I missed you in Tokyo.'

'I missed you, too, Jinx.'

'I'm sorry I didn't telephone or email you. I was exhausted and running the whole time I was there. I couldn't think straight. I bought you something.'

Jinx got up and walked over to the large white paper shopping bag. She pulled out a large, flat beautifully gift wrapped white box. She walked back and sat down next to Freya on the bed.

'I bought this in Kyoto. I hope you like it,' said Jinx and she smiled.

'I'm sure I will.'

Freya admired the white paper gift wrapping. It was really beautiful. Freya smiled and looked at Jinx. 'Thank you, Jinx. You didn't have to, but you did.'

Freya carefully unwrapped the gift to reveal a white cardboard box. She lifted the lid; white tissue paper. Freya paused. She looked at Jinx and smiled. Jinx smiled back. Okay—let's see what's inside…

Inside was a beautiful folded kimono. The dark blue (with white motifs) kimono had been carefully folded and placed in the box by the Kyoto shop. Freya placed the box on the white duvet and carefully lifted it up out of the box. It unfolded by itself as she lifted it up.

'It's beautiful. Thank you. I am speechless.'

'Akiko helped me order it. She knows the owner of the store in Kyoto. It should fit. I wrote down your dress and shirt sizes while in Northumberland. I looked at the labels in your wardrobe while you were out of the room. I picked the fabric myself. Two of the swimwear company staff drove me to Kyoto to pick it up the day before I left.'

Freya, still holding the kimono in her hands, looked at Jinx and smiled. 'I'm going to wear this to the party after the play. I will make a grand entrance.'

'I'm sure you will,' said Jinx.

And Jinx smiled.

THE WARM DORM ROOM
'Yes, well, I don't know. It's 9:15 and residence hall restrictions start at 11pm,' said Suga in her Scottish lilt. 'Yes, Jinx is back from Tokyo. She's about to bake a potato in my fireplace. Would you like to speak with her?'

Suga, holding the 1930s black Bakelite telephone receiver in one hand and the Bakelite rotary phone in the other, turned to Jinx and said, 'Jinx. Rex would like to speak with you.'

Jinx, still in her blue wool trousers and white cotton blouse looked in Suga's direction. She smiled, '*Rather!*' said Jinx excitedly. She walked over to Suga and carefully took the phone and receiver from her.

'Hello, Rex! How are you?!' said Jinx happily.

The phone lines at Midlands-Hasegawa, installed in the 1920s and upgraded in the 1940s, made every phone call seem like it was long distance circa 1950.

'It's so nice to hear your voice again, Jinx,' said Rex, his voice crackling down the phone line. Would you like to come over for tea? I'm here with Albert and Bramwell. I would like to hear about your trip to Japan.'

'Yes, yes, I would like that. I have so much I want to say to you, Rex,' said Jinx quietly and happily.

'Please come over now, if that's alright. We don't have long. Girls will be expelled from the men's residence hall at 11pm,' said Rex.

'That's alright. I turn into a pumpkin after 11pm anyway,' said Jinx happily. 'We will be right there.' Jinx then hung up the phone carefully and placed it back on the telephone stand in the corner.

'Rex, Albert, and Bramwell have invited us all to their rooms for tea. Who would like to go?'

REX'S AERIE
The girls (that is Jinx, Freya, Wren, Wallis, Suga, and Pasha) quickly put on their coats and shoes (while still wearing their pyjamas) and headed out the door. They walked quickly down the freezing and deserted hallways of the women's residence hall and out of the building and into the wintery night. The instant the cold hit them they broke into a sprint across the grass quad, the dead waxy leaves crunching under foot as they ran. And before they had made it half way a cross, the first white flakes of snow appeared.

'It's snowing,' said Jinx happily.

The girls all ran up the front steps and into the men's residence hall. The lobby was paneled in dark highly polished African hardwoods. The girls practically ran up the stairs through the icy cold of the unheated building until they reached Rex's door.

'I'll get it, said Albert. The nearly 6'3" Taiwanese undergraduate opened the glossy white door after hearing the polite knock. The girls were greeted by the sight of a Chinese giant. Albert moved to the side and the girls entered the warm room.

Albert was dressed in dark grey wool trousers, a white dress shirt, a dark blue padded jacket, and white slippers. His glossy black hair was cut more like a City banker than a typical undergraduate's. Albert was attractive. Bramwell wore a pair of navy blue trousers, a white button down dress shirt, a beige cricket sweater, and light grey slippers. Rex wore a pair of dark khaki trousers, a white button down dress shirt, a dark blue, v-neck wool sweater, and white slippers.

Rex's glossy blond hair seemed glossier than ever. He smiled. Rex was really cute. And his acting skills during the first dress rehearsal had made him extremely popular. And that Rex was a genuinely nice person made him even more popular.

'Rex, a word alone, please,' said Jinx as she entered the sitting room.

'Sure,' said Rex.

The girls gathered around the fireplace to warm themselves while Rex and Jinx went into the small bedroom attached to the sitting room. Jinx closed the door.

'Rex, I missed you so much during autumn break.'

'I missed you, too, Jinx.'

'Rex.' Jinx hesitated. How could she tell Rex that she loved him?

Rex stood in the dim light of the small bedroom. He waited for a moment unsure what to do.

'Rex?'

Yes.'

'I brought you something from Japan.'

(Jinx, why not just tell him? Jinx wanted to tell Rex how she really felt, but she couldn't. She was afraid. Did Rex love her too? Were they too young to know what love really was? Jinx knew that she loved Rex. She knew her love for Rex was true, but still, she hesitated.)

Jinx reached into her pocket and took out a small cardboard box decorated with Kanji and cherry blossoms. She held it out to Rex and said, 'It's Japanese candy, Rex. It's a mini box of chocolates with cherry jam centers. I bought them just for you.'

'Thank you, Jinx. How nice of you.'

'Have one,' said Jinx.

'Would you like one?' said Rex, as he opened the small, pink, and white, paper box.

'No. There aren't very many of them. I want you to have them. I bought them for you.'

'Thank you, Jinx. You are really sweet.'

Gemma—The Carthage Option—Waverly and Arthur

THE LAKE DISTRICT

The temporary bedroom—the former office of the 10th Baron—had been converted into Poppy and the twins' temporary bedroom. Two beds, one Poppy's large bed which had been disassembled and moved downstairs, and a single bed, had been placed next to each other. Just a few feet away were the twins' modern cribs. Poppy, shrouded in white Egyptian cotton sheets and a large white duvet, slept in the large bed, Violet in the other. Violet had had white cotton bedding sent to her from the Jacobean country house in Northumberland.

Violet had decided to stay with Poppy at the house in the Lake District until she departed for Midlands-Hasegawa to watch Freya and Jinx in the play just before the Christmas holiday. Poppy's health was still fragile. Violet had stayed to monitor and help Poppy. And help with the infant twins.

Holly, the young English nanny, was staying in the former billiards room thirty feet away. The billiards table had been pushed towards the back of the room and a single bed placed in the billiards room along with a several plastic bins of clothing, boxes of disposable diapers, and an array of baby shampoo, soap, and an endless list of other things. Holly was only twenty years old, but she had attended a training course (at the 12th Baron's expense) and had also helped raise her younger siblings. The family had known Holly since she had been a baby herself. She was sweet and reliable. And the 12th Baron had personally selected her to care for his infant grandchildren. Holly wore a dark blue uniform (with a large white collar) and when outside, a straw hat with a dark blue ribbon. It was the uniform of her lesser known nanny college.

Poppy was deeply touched when Violet had offered to stay with her. She was also grateful. She appreciated having one of her closest friends with her. And Violet was healthy; Poppy's elderly parents were not. The events surrounding the birth of the twins had taken a toll on both of them. Poppy was worried about them.

Helen had her own twins, Lucy and Henry, to look after. James, Poppy's older brother, would be visiting this weekend. That would be nice. James would help too.

The Croatian housemaids were both days away from departing for the

Christmas holidays in Croatia. The paid holiday was a reward for Kata's miraculous discovery of Poppy that fateful night. Marija had also always been loyal and hardworking too. It was only right they both get to go home for Christmas and see their loved ones. James and Brian were both usually away in the City. Two local girls had been hired to work in December and January as temporary replacements. They had worked part-time for the family before, usually working behind the counter of the small tourist center next to the castle.

Poppy was happy. She had finally given birth to her son and daughter. Both were blonde and blue eyed like Poppy. A nurse had also been hired to help with the infant twins. The doctors visited once a day to check on both Poppy and the twins. The country house was a whirl of excitement and semi-turmoil now. The young nurse slept on a cot next to Holly's bed.

Poppy had lost a lot of weight. She was relieved to be rapidly returning to her normal weight. Poppy, a diminutive 5' 3", was now able to walk and move around easily. Poppy usually wore loose fitting pyjamas and cashmere jumpers. When she went for a walk outside, she wore the purple wool cashmere cape (with a mink collar) that Gula had had made for her at Vahtra. Poppy loved the purple cape. She loved the color and the person who had had it made for her.

Poppy's morning routine consisted of a hot shower (there was no bathtub on the first floor of the house) and breakfast with the family in the dining room. Violet would always join her. Holly and the nurse would stay with the wins in the temporary bedroom and had breakfast after Poppy had returned. Poppy would then breastfeed the twins (again) and place then back in their cribs. She would sing to them softly and gently stroke their hair for a while. Violet would sometimes join her. Violet had a beautiful singing voice. And to everyone's surprise—especially Violet's—Vava's maternal instincts had appeared. Violet was a good mother to the twins. Why hadn't she been one to her own daughter Freya? It was while helping Poppy with the newborn twins that Violet realized what she had missed out on with Freya. She also realized how demanding motherhood really was; how hard Gemma and Karmen (the Croat nanny) had worked to raise Freya without her. And why Freya had grown to love them both for it.

These tiny little beings, so fragile and dependent, needed motherly affection and love to protect them and raise them. Poppy had found joy in her children: a happiness she had almost given up on ever experiencing.

THE DRAWING ROOM

'Poppy, you are well on your way to recovery, but please take care. No unnecessary exertions. You still need time to heal. Eat healthy, balanced meals and go for short walks, weather permitting,' said the aged and white-haired doctor.

'Yes. Thank you, Doctor. I feel stronger every day. Thank you for driving out to the house to see me.'

'I'm happy to do it. The twins are beautiful and healthy, Poppy. I think you should consider staying downstairs for a few months. The staircase would be a lot for you and the twins to go up and down several times a day. The office is a large space. It's suitable for the time being. You might want to see about installing a bathtub downstairs.'

'I think you're right,' said the 12th Baron. 'I will have Hector look into it today. We could order one and have it installed this week.'

'That sounds heavenly,' said Poppy.

'An acrylic bathtub is lightweight and easy to install,' said the baron.

'The village doctor will be by later to check on the twins,' said the doctor.

THE TEMPORARY BEDROOM

'Waverly smiled at me,' said Violet quietly. Violet was sitting on her narrow bed and holding her infant goddaughter in her arms. Violet smiled. Today Violet was clad in dark grey wool trousers, a pale blue cashmere v-neck sweater, and white slippers. Her long, glossy blonde hair had been tied back with a pale blue ribbon.

'She loves you, Vava,' said Poppy. 'Arthur likes looking at me. Sometimes he smiles too. He is so beautiful and sweet. The twins both sleep well. Oh,

Arthur is smiling at me. Yes, I love you, Arthur. Mummy loves you.'

Outside the winds picked up. The overcast sky suddenly grew darker and a minute later a snowflake appeared. And then another. And another. The snow fell lightly and within minutes a thin layer of snow was blanketing the grounds outside the house.

'Look, Arthur, snow,' said Poppy quietly and she gently caressed Arthur soft cheek.

'Yes, Waverly, that is snow. Northern girls like us soon get used to it,' said Violet happily.

THE VILLAGE
'Yes, I'm looking for a former Royal Air Force training center. It's supposed to be somewhere around here,' asked the man in accented English. (Where was this person from? It was difficult to tell.) He was holding a paper road map.

'It's a few miles away. If you take the road here, you should be there in about twenty five minutes. It's just off to the left. There are several old redbrick buildings. Why do you ask?'

'Well, I'd prefer you not tell anyone else, but I am an estate agent. A client is interested in it.'

'The old RAF training center? It was a furniture mill for decades. The original owner passed away a couple of years ago and his daughter sold it. I haven't been out in that direction in years. I can't imagine the buildings are in very good condition,' said the village local.

'Well, with property prices what they are, my client is willing to invest a little to save a lot,' said the stranger.

'Well, good on him, if he can,' said the villager.

'There is only one road to it?' asked the stranger.

'Yes. Not many people live out there.'

Gemma—The Carthage Option—Lunch in the City

LONDON
The City continued to lurch from one financial crisis to another. And most of the upheaval had remained hidden from the general public—and the investors. Secrecy was paramount. It was other hedge funds that were losing money, not yours. No, don't worry. Your money is safe.

Only it wasn't.

The people (or person) behind all of the market disruptions were (or was) still unknown. And this is what worried everyone the most. Was it a government or a rogue group or individual behind all of this? And to what end? Was this just looting? Or was there more to it?

THE CITY
Gemma had not seen Enoch since she had return to London. Five days had passed. Enoch would call her at 10pm every evening and say goodnight. Only Enoch was never at home. He was always at his office.

Gemma's schedule had stabilized somewhat and she found herself leaving the office at 8pm every evening. Isolde would arrive at 7:30pm, and after being briefed by Gemma, would take over the running of the office. Isolde was extremely professional and reliable. She was never late and worked extremely hard. Gemma was happy to have her.

Alexa was a physical wreck. The morning Gemma had appeared in the office after returning from the Lake District, she had found Alexa asleep on her sofa with dark circles around her eyes and wearing wrinkled clothing. Gemma returned to her desk until she heard Alexa's alarm clock go off. A moment later Alexa had emerged from her office. When she saw Gemma she smiled faintly and asked her to come into her office. Gemma had never seen Alexa in that condition before, and it worried her.

'Alexa, how long has it been since you have slept in a proper bed?' asked Gemma.

Alexa smiled weakly and said, 'Three days.'

'Perhaps it's not my place to say this, but, as a friend, and office manager, perhaps you should go home and get some sleep? Jemima and Tarquin arrived an hour ago. They've had a full night's sleep. I'm here now and Allegra and the others will be coming in later this evening. We will call if anything happens.'

Alexa smiled. 'Thank you, Gemmy. You're right. I do need to get some proper sleep.'

THE CITY

Gemma walked through the City, London's financial district, observing everything around her. The grey, cold, overcast day invigorated her. The cold made her feel alive. Gemma's tousled brown hair blew in the wind as she made her way down the pavement. She looked at her silver Cartier wristwatch: 11:45am.

Gemma caught a glimpse of herself in the window of a shop a she walked. She slowed as she passed by the Victorian store front and surreptitiously observed her reflection (didn't everyone?) in the glass. The slim and diminutive Gemma looked quite professional in her tailored coat. More than a year had passed since she had met Grey that rainy day in September. More than a year had passed since that traumatizing night in October in Primrose Hill. Gemma's life had changed completely. Gemma had changed. Gemma had been forced to change repeatedly through all of the shocks and reversals that had taken place throughout her life. All the people who had tormented her, had, for the most part, gone unpunished. It wasn't fair. But Gemma had found Enoch, and he truly loved her.

The people who had tormented Gemma had disappeared. Where were they now? The 5th rate, haggish, repulsive, and bomb shaped assistant office manager that had gleefully informed Gemma that she had been made redundant at the magazine was now jobless herself and living in

Bournemouth on benefits. Gemma's husband George, the 5th Baron, had left England years ago; where he was he now, Gemma didn't know, and she didn't want to know. The classmates at All Saints and Oxford who had supported her had gone on to have successful careers and, for the most part, happy lives. The classmates, who had turned on her and abandoned her, had disappeared. They no longer appeared in the pages of Tatler or the Daily Telegraph. Their presence in London had faded away with their youth. What had happened to their dreams? Perhaps their quick descent into obscurity and an empty life were punishment enough? Gemma really didn't have an answer to that question. She was grateful to have found true friends and finally, someone who loved her as much as she loved him.

Gemma crossed the street and looked back at the large glass office building at 30 St Mary's Axe. What a fantastic structure. It was the only modern structure in London that Gemma actually liked. And, to Gemma, it represented her new life. Gemma looked at the red aviation warning lights as they glowed in the wintery gloom. How beautiful.

Ping.

Gemma looked at her smartphone.

I've reserved a table for us near the window. I'll be there in five minutes. –Enoch.

Gemma smiled. She put her phone back in her coat pocket and continued on to the restaurant.

THE RESTAURANT
The Hungarian restaurant, its red walls adorned with Attila coats and silver framed faded photographs and gilt framed portraits of Hungarian hussars of the former Austro-Hungarian Empire, was warm and inviting. The cold was left outside as Gemma entered the crowded main room. The owner recognized her—not as the future Mrs Tara, but as Gemma Ripley, a friend of the 'dangerously cute' Poppy Atherton. Gemma gave her cashmere coat to the dark-haired coat girl who carefully hung it up in the cloak room.

'Good afternoon, Madam Ripley', said the grey and white haired owner. 'It's nice to see you again.'

'Thank you, sir. It's nice to see you.'

'How is Madam Atherton? Has she had her baby yet?'

'Yes. Twins. A boy and girl. They are beautiful.'

'How wonderful. Please tell Madam Atherton that I am happy for her.'

Gemma smiled. 'Thank you. I will tell her. Poppy misses you and this restaurant. It is her favorite. And it's my favorite too.'

The elderly Hungarian smiled and bowed slightly. 'I have your table. Mr Tara asked that you both be seated near the window. Please, right this way.'

Gemma put on her tortoise shell reading glasses and looked at the menu. Gemma read the selections carefully. Gemma smiled. She knew what she would order before she left the offices of Millennium Investments; what Gemma usually ordered: steak. Gemma enjoyed reading the menu.

'Am I late?' asked Enoch.

Enoch, in a dark grey suit, white dress shirt, and blue, red, and grey tartan neck tie, was handsome. His glossy brown hair had been freshly cut like a City banker, and he was, as always, clean shaven. At 5'9", the slender Enoch looked every bit the City banker he was. Gemma smiled as she looked at him. No. While the was a sophisticated air about him, he didn't appear to be the financial warlord that he truly was. No, the 'Mysterious Mr Tara' remained a mystery—even to Gemma.

Gemma looked at her silver watch and smiled. 'No, you are right on time.'

Enoch was given a thin leather bound menu by the waitress. He read through it, occasionally looking up from the menu in contemplation. When the waitress appeared, Gemma ordered steak (medium well) and Enoch ordered a salad. He wanted something light that day.

Gemma wanted to ask Enoch how work was going, but she didn't. They worked at different firms. Their business lives had to be kept separate. Both of them understood that. The elephant in the room was the unfolding disaster raging just beneath the glassy surface of the financial world.

'Gemma, I'm free this weekend. Well, I'm taking time off from work. If you have time, would you like to visit Poppy?'

'Yes, I would love to, Enoch. We could stay at my country house.'

'Yes, I would like that. What time do you finish work?' asked Enoch.

'These days, 8pm. You?'

'Eight o'clock sounds about right. Please pack and bring your suitcase with you to the office. I'll pick you up and we can head directly to the train station.'

QUADRIGA INVESTMENTS

Carter Holland smiled. It was all so easy. Much easier than he thought it would be. Money was being drained from the system at every level, and yet, Carter remained unconnected to it all. No one suspected anything. Well, at least not that he could tell. And Carter Holland's inner circle was actively searching for any signs of detection or awareness. No, so far, Carter was attacking unseen.

Carter, in a crisp white dress shirt, black suit, and silver silk tie, examined himself in the mirror in the white tiled bathroom in his private office. He was handsome. And he knew it. Yes, at fifty-two, Carter had retained his looks. It hadn't been easy. His exercise regimen and diet were strict. Life requires discipline, if one is to attain what one really wants.

Carter walked back into the white walled office. The minimalist offices of Quadriga Investments were nearly blinding against the darkening skies of London in winter. Blinding? Or perhaps they shone like a beacon? Yes, against the decay of England, Quadriga Investments was a light fighting the darkness.

Carter swiveled in the modern leather chair. He looked out of the top floor window of his office. In the distance he could see the rocket shaped structure at 30 St Mary Axe. The building no longer stared back at him. The Gherkin glowed translucently against the grey sky. The glassy structure suddenly appeared fragile to him. Carter felt like he could shatter it with one well-placed blow.

The key to destroying Enoch Tara was there inside the 12th floor offices of a minor investment firm. Timing would be important. Carter had to strike at the right moment. Carter had already mapped it all out in his mind.

The human mind—what a wonder. The universe's greatest gift to mankind had been the human mind. And yet, it was easily the most unappreciated gift that had ever been bestowed. How many really used it? Virtually no one. Carter's mind was all he really had. It was all anyone really had. Carter had always known that. Carter read everything he could. That 'knowledge was power' was no cliché to Carter Holland. No, the mind's abilities were infinite, boundless. If one chose to waste their mind's potential, whose fault was that? Only theirs. Only yours.

Carter walked to one of the windows of the Edwardian bank building that housed his investment firm. None of what he could see from the window of his office really mattered anymore. Soon, very soon, he would escape this rotting city and leave everyone behind. What fate would befall these people didn't matter. They had done nothing while their country faded away. They had been passive. They had not gone into the trenches and waged war. They had accepted defeat. They had humiliated themselves and disgraced their homeland. Carter owed them nothing. And soon, they too would fade away. Forgotten. It was only fair.

Gemma—The Carthage Option—The Country House

THE LAKE DISTRICT

The train pulled into the station a few minutes before midnight. It was

34

snowing lightly; a thin layer of snow covered the Lake District. Enoch had been met at the small train station near Poppy's family pile by a dark blue 2019 Range Rover driven by two of his security team. The suited and booted former British Paras had placed Gemma and Enoch's luggage in the back of the SUV and driven them to Gemma's country house twenty minutes away from the station.

The vehicles headlights cut through the icy darkness as it moved down the nearly empty, snow covered country roads. Gemma and Enoch held hands the entire way.

THE FORMER ROYAL AIR FORCE TRAINING CENTER

The Range Rover arrived at the house and soon a white BMW appeared with three more members of the security detail. They would spend the night patrolling the grounds of the house. (Unbeknownst to Gemma, Enoch had purchased the rest of the land and buildings around her. He didn't want to worry about troublesome neighbors.)

A small Nissen hut (erected in 1939), a hundred yards away from the Gemma's house and hidden behind some tall trees, was now a makeshift office for the security teams. The men guarding Mr Tara would take turns sleeping on one of the camp beds or drinking coffee. And taking some time out between patrols to warm themselves near one of the electric room heaters. And no, Enoch hadn't told Gemma about the security hut, not yet.

Gemma turned on the lights behind the white plaster Egyptian hieroglyphics and ancient Greek letters of the crown molding as they entered the main room. The lights behind the plasterwork cast long shadows and partially illuminated the room. The hardwood floors gleamed around them.

'You'll room across the hall from me,' said Gemma. 'Knock on my door if you need anything.'

Gemma opened the door of the small white walled bedroom and showed Enoch inside. The single bed with its white Egyptian cotton sheets, white pillows and tartan patterned wool blankets beckoned.

'Thank you, Gem. See you tomorrow morning.'

'I'll make us breakfast. Do you like pancakes? Of course you do,' said Gemma and she smiled.

Gemma, beautiful , slender, kind, and fragile, was home. This mid-sized red brick building was hers. She owned it. It was Gemma's. A person needs a space they can call their own. Gemma, having been adrift for so long, had finally found a place she could call her own, and Gemma, at forty-one, (almost forty-two) was infinitely grateful to have found it. Mars had also helped her by asking the real estate development company he worked for to lower the price of the building so that Gemma could afford to buy it. Yes, Gemma was aware of that, and she was grateful for that too.

Gemma walked into her bedroom. She closed the glossy white door. Space was at a premium in the two bedrooms in her 'country house'. Gemma's bedroom, which was considerably larger than the guest bedroom, had a small double size bed (with a Mid-Century Modern wooden headboard), a Mid-Century Modern, wardrobe with a splayed frame, double doors, rounded edges, and linear design, a nightstand, and a narrow Mid-Century Modern dresser. A modern mirror had been attached to the wall above the dresser; if Gemma stood next to the nightstand, she could see her full length reflection.

The wardrobe held a three white cotton blouses, three sets of country tweeds, a dark blue hunt coat, two pairs of beige jodhpurs, two blue blazers, two dresses, three pairs of wool trousers, two skirts, and waterproof dark blue wool cape. The two large drawers in the wardrobe contained several pairs of denim blue jeans, and three sweaters (including her beige All Saints v-neck cricket sweater).

The narrow 4-drawer dresser next to the bedroom contained the rest of her clothing, which included several sets of cotton and flannel pyjamas. One of her black velvet hunt caps rested on top of the wooden dresser next to a hunt whip.

Gemma still kept her fur hood from Holland and Holland at Poppy's family pile as well as at her semi-detached in Covent Garden. She also had clothes at Violet's house in London and at the houses of other friends across England. Gemma had decided to keep her wardrobe scatted about, as it is what had saved her from losing her entire wardrobe to the bailiffs. Gemma's collection of shoes and boots were also stored in houses across the country. Gemma didn't keep any clothing at Enoch's.

Gemma kept several pairs of rubber boots, shoes, and leather riding boots in a narrow room adjacent to the entrance to her home.

Gemma turned on the lamp on the nightstand. No, not bright enough. She turned on the lights in the bedroom. She stood in front of the mirror and examined her reflection. He complexion was clear, smooth, and youthful. Yes, a proper diet, skincare, and exercise had kept her looking youthful. She tilted her head to one side and then the other. Yes, still beautiful. **In spite of everything.** Gemma noticed a few more silver strands of hair in glossy brown hair and bangs which framed her face. That was alright.

Gemma undressed, put on a white waffle patterned bathroom, and walked out of her bedroom and down to the white tiled bathroom to take a shower before going to bed.

THE FAMILY PILE

Mars, in dark khaki trousers, a white dress shirt, and a blue blazer stood as Poppy entered the drawing room. Poppy, three weeks since giving birth, had lost almost all of the weight she had gained while carrying the twins. Buttoned up in a pair of rum colored trousers and wearing a white cotton blouse (with open cuffs and a large collar), the flaxen haired and 'dangerously cute' Poppy smiled as she greeted Mars.

'I'm happy to see you, Mars. Please, have a seat.'

Mars sat down in one of the purple Art Deco chairs, opposite the purple (with lavender piping) Art Deco sofa where Poppy was now seated.

'Mars, you have been a brother to me since I was thirteen. And Father told me all that you did for us when I was in the hospital. And I love you for it. We all do. Mars, I have asked Gemma to be Godmother to my son Arthur. I plan to ask Enoch to be one of the Godfathers. I would you to be the other. It would mean a lot to me if you accepted,' said Poppy quietly.

Mars, caught entirely by surprise, could only stare blankly for a moment. Then the wave hit and Mars' expression softened. Deeply moved, Mars spoke. 'Thank you, Poppy. This means a lot to me. And yes.'

THE BALLROOM

Gemma and Enoch were led to the large ballroom by Marija, one of the black-uniformed Croat housemaids. Marija had spoken to Gemma in Croatian in the entry hall. Yes, in four days she would fly home to Croatia. 'Yes, Mrs Atherton, Mrs Maud, and the twins are in the ballroom.'

Marija opened the double doors and Gemma and Enoch entered the ballroom. The cavernous ballroom was filled with natural light. Placed in the sunlight which poured from the windows on the far side of the room were several folding wooden chairs that looked like they belonged on the deck of the Titanic, not in an English country house in the Lake District. Reclining in the deck chairs and sunning themselves in the warm sunshine were Violet and Poppy. Violet and Poppy, both clad in wool and cashmere, looked in their direction and both smiled.

'Gemmy!' said Poppy happily. 'And you brought Enoch, what a nice surprise.'

Violet stood up and helped Poppy get up out of the deck chair. Violet, blonde, blue eyed, and radiantly beautiful, looked better than she had while a teenager at All Saints.

Enoch smiled. He was happy to see Poppy looking so healthy and happy. Gemma and Enoch walked across the ballroom and met the now slender mother of twins.

'You look great, Poppy,' said Enoch happily.

'Enoch, please, let me introduce you to the twins. Please come with me,' said Poppy.

While Gemma hugged Violet, Poppy led Enoch into the temporary bedroom. Holly, the young blue-uniformed brunette nanny stood to greet them. She smiled and bowed slightly. Holly took a few steps towards Poppy, stopped in front of her and said very quietly, 'They are fast asleep, ma'am.'

'Thank you, Holly. Please take a break. I would like to introduce Mr Tara to my twins.'

Holly bowed slightly and departed. After she had left the room, Poppy quietly closed the glossy white door to the bedroom. Enoch hovered over the cribs. The little twins were angelic. Beautiful and adorable at the same time. Enoch smiled.

'Yes, as Gemma said, beautiful like their mother.'

Poppy smiled. 'Enoch. I have asked Gemma to be Godmother to Arthur. She is my dearest friend. And you have made her happy. You love her as much as she loves you. And I love you for it. I would like you and Gemmy to be Godparents to Arthur. I wanted to ask you privately.'

Enoch smiled, his innocent nature emerging into the open. 'Thank you, Poppy. I would love to. And to share the honor and responsibility with Gemma, my soon-to-be.'

'Mars will be co-Godfather with you,' said Poppy quietly, so as not to wake the twins.

'Even better,' replied Enoch. 'We could both train him in the ways of finance,' said Enoch, and he smiled.

THE DINING ROOM

The white-haired 12th Baron sat at the head of the table with Mars, the 13th Baron, seated at is right. Enoch was seated on his left. At the other end of the table was the baroness, Poppy, Violet, Helen, and Gemma. The lunch, served on white bone china, was welcome on the cold day in December. Edward, the family chef, had prepared beef stew, mashed potatoes, steamed vegetables, fresh garlic bread, and rice pilaf. The black-uniformed Croat housemaids served the meals flawlessly.

'Waverly and Arthur sleep soundly. You and your brother James were both light sleepers,' said the baroness.

'That must be Brian's DNA at work,' laughed Poppy cheerfully.

'I look forward to teaching them how to play cricket,' said the 12th Baron.

'Yes, Henry and Lucy could play with cricket with them in the castle,' said Helen.

'I'm going to buy them cricket whites as soon as they can walk,' said Gemma happily. 'Arthur will captain the team at Eton. For sure.'

'I am so happy to have all of you here,' said the baroness. Poppy's mother had maintained her attractiveness. Her white hair was rested on her shoulders. The baroness smiled. 'This will be quite the Christmas with all of the children. Yes, I am looking forward to it.'

'James telephoned and said he had arranged to have an entire week off this year,' said Helen.

The baroness smiled. 'I know James would like to be here more often with you and the children, Helen. I'm glad he will get to spend the holidays with us.'

'What are your holiday plans, Violet?' asked the baroness.

'We are going to watch Freya perform on stage at Midlands-Hasegawa and then take the train back to Northumberland. The entire family is gathering at the house this year. It will be nice, I'm sure.'

'Please tell you parents I said "hello". It has been ages since we met. Far too long. We will have to meet them this winter,' said the baroness.

'Yes, we would love to have you at the house,' replied Violet. Violet's parents were older then Poppy's, and far more frail. They had been friends for decades. Life had separated them.

'Mars, if you don't have any plans, please do join us this year. We could all attend church services at St George's together,' said the baroness.

'Thank you. I will be here. I am happiest here with the family in the Lake District,' said Mars.

The baroness smiled.

'Gemma, what are your Christmas plans?' asked the baroness.

'Well, I will take the train to Midlands-Hasegawa with Enoch to watch Freya in the play. Jubal Wyatt, the American playwright who wrote the play, will travel with us from London. Afterwards, Jubal will return to London to spend Christmas with friends. I will take the train back to the Lake District with Enoch. We're going to stay at my country house.'

'You are both welcome to spend Christmas with us,' said the baroness.

'Yes,' said the baron. 'And I'm sure all of the grandchildren would like to see you too.'

'Thank you, sir. Yes, we will come by. I love Christmas here with the family,' said Gemma happily.

THE BALLROOM
Two of Enoch's security team, in coat and tie, sat in folding chairs at a folding table and enjoyed lunch with the nurse. Holly was in the office watching over the twins. They were served the same meal as the family. They both ate heartily.

The athletic and slender former Paras also enjoyed speaking with the attractive Croatian housemaids who served them lunch and the young blonde nurse seated across from them.

After the nurse had finished lunch, she exchanged places with Holly. And the two young security men happily talked with the attractive young nanny.

THE TEMPORARY BEDROOM

Outside the family pile, a light snow fell. Soon the grounds around the house and castle ruins were blanketed in a thin layer of snow.

Inside the warm bedroom, Violet held Waverly in her arms and cooed over the tiny infant. Gemma, sitting on the edge of Poppy's large bed, held Arthur. Gemma smiled often, and every time she did, little Arthur smiled back.

Poppy leaned back in the old worn leather chair in the corner of the room. Poppy was content to watch her friends gently and carefully hold her children. Her only regret was that Gemma had been unable to conceive. Gemma was a natural mother, a good mother. It wasn't fair. So much in life is unfair. And the kindest suffer the most. Poppy was happy that she had made Gemma Arthur's Godmother. Gemma would always be there for him—for both of her children. That was a comforting thought. Poppy knew Gemma would protect and nurture them.

Holly and the nurse were in the billiards room playing billiards. The table had been placed at an awkward angle, but that had only served to make the game more interesting. Eventually, once Poppy had recovered fully, the nanny would move into the nursery upstairs with the children.

The baron, baroness, and Helen were in the drawing room; Mars and Enoch were in the library.

Henry and Lucy would soon return from the village school. Helen would pick them up in the baron's silver 1975 Bristol 411 motorcar.

'Waverly is becoming fidgety again,' said Violet quietly.

'Yes, it's time to breastfeed them,' said Poppy.' Please lock the door. I don't want the men walking in on me,' said Poppy and she smiled.

THE LIBRARY

The library was at one end of the house and the plaster patterned ceiling relief hovered two storeys above the visitors. The white ceiling contrasted nicely with the grey stone of the walls. The ancient stone used to construct the walls of the house had all come from the ruins of the family castle.

The first storey of the room was filled with wall mounted book shelves. The second storey of the room was filled with large windows. The wall on the front of the house also had large windows as did the far end. The back wall of the house was windowless and had been left bare so that a tapestry could be hung from it.

The richly embroidered tapestry depicted a group of knights on armoured warhorses charging into battle in the ancient Kingdom of Jerusalem. Latin words had also been embroidered onto the wall hanging. A few medieval weapons and shields decorated the walls of the library, and in one corner, there stood a suit of medieval armor.

There were two large tables in the library and several high-back chairs. The library was filled with thousands of books. Many of the really old books were kept in a glass case near the tapestry.

Mars and Enoch stood in front of the ancient tapestry. Enoch wore a white button down dress shirt and the same dark khaki trousers and brown leather oxfords he had purchased at a small clothing shop last summer while visiting Oxford University with Gemma. He liked wearing the clothing he had worn that weekend. He had been wearing this clothing the first time Gemma had kissed him in the garden maze.

'Yes, it's almost a thousand years old, not a reproduction. It's best if you ask Poppy about it. She knows its history better than anyone,' said Mars.

Enoch read the Latin embroidered on the tapestry out loud. He slowly deciphered the Latin words into English. Mars helped him.

'Interesting,' said Enoch quietly. Enoch then became lost in thought for a moment.

Mars moved closer, and examined the finer details of the wall hanging carefully. When he turned around, Enoch was staring at him. It was obvious to Mars that Enoch wanted to talk to him about something. What? It must be what was going on in the markets. Yes, Mars had been paying close attention to it.

'May I ask you something?' asked Enoch.

'Yes.'

'It's about what is going on in the City.'

'I assumed it would be along those lines,' replied Mars.

'If you don't want to answer, you don't have to,' said Enoch.

'Alright.'

'Who do you think is behind all of this?' asked Enoch as he folded his arms.

Mars was standing in front of the large medieval tapestry. It was quite the backdrop. Mars appeared to be an actor on stage performing a soliloquy. Mars, his brown hair peppered with white and silver hairs, and wearing a pair of dark grey wool trousers and a white dress shirt (with a St James collar), black leather dress shoes, and his silver Omega watch still looked like the former hedge fund manager he once was. And as Enoch was soon to discover, Mars was still as brilliant and insightful as ever. A single miscalculation had led to his downfall in Hong Kong.

'I have some ideas. I think you do too,' said Mars. 'It's definitely someone in the City.'

Enoch listened in silence. His facial expression remained one of intense focus.

'Whoever it is, is within the Square Mile,' said Mars.

'Could it be one person or a group of people?' asked Enoch.

'I don't know. If it is purely for financial gain, then it is probably a small and tightly knit group of people. And they know how to cover their tracks. They know that if found out they would spend the rest of their lives in prison.'

'And if it were an individual?' asked Enoch.

'Then I suspect there would be a much different set of motives behind all of this. Financial, yes. But also political.'

'How so?' asked Enoch.

'This is looting on an unprecedented scale. And it is highly destructive to the global economy. To what end? I would say some sort of political objective is in play,' said Mars.

Enoch exhaled. He was quiet for a moment.

'What political objectives could be achieved by all of this?'

'That is something that I have been pondering too. It's easy to lose the plot in all of this. One shouldn't let their minds wander too far,' replied Mars.

'Let your mind wander for a moment, Mars. I would be grateful for any insights.'

Mars began to pace slowly back and forth in front of the tapestry. He stopped, folded his arms, and then raised one hand to his chin. 'It's either destroying nations or building new ones.'

Enoch held his breath for a moment and then exhaled. 'Yes. Yes. Exactly. That's what I have come away with too. Someone is trying to provoke revolution and the destruction of the country—or countries. Either seeking a change in government or the political system, or, as you have suggested, create new countries or a new federation of countries. Crisis forces change. And that kind of change is usually not good.'

'No, it isn't. Perhaps they are trying to provoke a war? That would accelerate everything. To what end? It's only speculation on my part,' said Mars.

'Why are you convinced it is someone within the City?' asked Enoch.

'I have been examining the cash flows and subtle movements in the markets. They are very well hidden. Very well hidden. But, I have spent the last week holed up in my house going through everything. Most of the activity is emanating from London. I have traced some of it out. All of the documentation is attached to every free bit of space on my office walls at home. I can show it to you, if have the time.'

'I have the time, Mars. Could we drive over to your house now? Gemma and the others are with the children today. How far away do you live?'

'About twenty, twenty-five minutes away,' said Mars.

Enoch then refocused and observed Mars standing in front of the ancient tapestry. Enoch smiled. 'Mars, I like your backdrop.'

Mars turned around to face the tapestry. He smiled and said, with his back to Enoch, 'Why yes. It is rather dramatic. Isn't it?'

2 THE JANISSARIES

Gemma—The Carthage Option—Muddy Hills

MIDLANDS-HASEGAWA UNIVERSITY

'Yes, my family owns a farm in Northumberland. I like farming. It's tough work, but I enjoy being outdoors and the land has been in my family for hundreds of years. I want to contribute to England. My father is quite innovative. He has published several books and articles on farming and agriculture,' said Bramwell in his posh intonation.

Suga smiled. 'Yes, my father is a farmer too. He has one your father's books on his bookshelf in our library. My father thinks your father is brilliant. I have actually read a few chapters of the book and three of the Baron's articles in agricultural journals. My father recommended them to me.'

Bramwell smiled brightly. Never before had he heard anyone his age speak of his father in glowing terms. Yes, Suga, the beautiful Scottish undergraduate from a few miles north of The Borders admired Bram's father, the 11th Baron.

'Do you plan to become a farmer one day?'

'Yes, eventually. My father is only 42. He retired after twenty years in the

Paras and now runs the farm with my grandparents. I'm an only child. There is no one else. I will never sell the land. My father is renovating a pele tower right now. He says that when it is complete, I can use it as my own private refuge,' said Suga in her Scottish lilt.

The blonde and curvaceous Suga had heavy eyelids which often made her look bored and indifferent. She was far from it most of the time. Suga was also rather intelligent, even academic. Suga (Ava) was also a talented actress. Her small role in the play had confirmed that to everyone. Even Freya was impressed. And she was talking to Bram.

'Yes, I love living in the Scottish Marches,' said Ava. 'I am descended from Border Rievers. We still own several swords, saddles, and bits of armour. They are all in the library. I know my house must seem grand to you the way I talk about it, but it is rather modest. And I love it. I live there with my parents and grandparents. My family owns 382 acres. We grow vegetables and have dairy cows. My family owns a small dairy. We bottle milk to sell locally. My family still owns a dairy cart from 1902.'

'Ah, well, we have no less than three pele towers on our farm that were built to deter you. However, you are always welcome to visit us with your family, Ava.'

'One day, perhaps, we will visit.'

'The pele towers are all in ruins, but they are still interesting to explore. We also have dairy cows, sheep, and horses. I have a horse named Barely that I ride when I can. My younger sisters ride him several times a week. Barley gets lonely easily and enjoys exercise. My father is an excellent equestrian. He was an officer in the Coldstream Guards. One day, I will serve in the regiment too. Just a short service commission. I want to return to the farm.'

Suga (Ava) smiled. 'Bram, you are much more interesting than I thought you would be.'

Bramwell smiled. Yes, in the last twenty four hours he had managed to make new friends and possibly—just possibly—find a girlfriend.

THE MARBLE FIREPLACE

Freya and Wallis, their teeth chattering, both warmed themselves by the fire. They had taken off their shoes and now stood in their wool socks, pyjamas, and coats—Freya in a blue quilted jacket, Wallis in a dark blue parka. Outside, the snow was falling steadily.

'It will be a blizzard by the time we return to our hall,' said Wallis through chattering teeth.

'Yes, we might have to stay here tonight,' said Freya and she smiled.

'Well, at 11pm they come around and check the rooms; where will we hide you all?' asked Albert.

'We can all pile into the bedroom and wait until after 11pm,' said Freya.

Albert looked at Freya for a moment. Was she serious?

Freya smiled. 'Don't worry, Albert. I'm only teasing, you *thrilling bore*,' said Freya in her posh intonation.

Albert wasn't sure what a 'thrilling bore' was, but he was relieved that he wouldn't have to explain to his family in Taiwan why he had been expelled from Midlands-Hasegawa.

Wren sat down on the dark blue sofa and looked around the sitting room. The white Christmas lights over the fireplace along with the two St George pennant flags were nice touches. The twinkling white lights also drew attention to the clear glass vase on the mantlepiece filled with red, blue, and purple paper tulips. Wren assumed (correctly) that Rex had made them. On the wall opposite the white sash windows was a poster of a painting of a young Queen Elizabeth II in military uniform. Yes, Queen Elizabeth II was beautiful. Wren bowed her head slightly to the monarch. Yes, For Queen and Country—always.

Wren, the honey blonde 'Hon' from Mercia, then noticed that Jinx and Rex were missing. She looked at the closed bedroom door and smiled. Wren had noticed Rex at the Rhodesia Club meetings. He was a model of epicene beauty. Yes, Wren had noticed him, but he wasn't a Hon. Now she regretted not approaching him months earlier. Rex, flaxen haired and with the slender build and bearing of a ballet dancer, was beautiful; that Suga, Freya, and Jinx had all spoken of his immense talent and good looks, had made Rex all even more beautiful in Wren's eyes. Alas, Rex belonged to Jinx now. Well, if not Jinx, then someone else. Perhaps Wren could...No.

The tiny and delicate Pashay started to speak with the towering Albert in Mandarin Chinese. Albert smiled. He gestured slightly and said something in Chinese, and Pasha took a seat in one of the wooden chairs near the fireplace. Albert sat down opposite her and they began to speak quietly and happily.

Wren didn't think they made Chinese that tall.

Freya sat on the window ledge and looked out across the quad. It was snowing; the cloisters of the girls' residence halls could barely be made out through the falling snow and darkness. Muddy Hills was beautiful. And it was a safe place for free speech and debate. That made Midlands-Hasegawa University even more beautiful than Oxford University. The forgotten Midlands-Hasegawa was spiritually pure. Freya, deep in thought, didn't hear the bedroom door open and Jinx and Rex emerge.

Rex and Jinx made their way to the fireplace and spoke with Suga and Bram. Suga smiled. Jinx modelled her new haircut for Suga. 'It looks really nice, Jinx. Of course, I would never cut my hair. My hair is meant to be long,' said Suga.

Wren stood up and walked over to Freya who was still looking out the window. Freya's blonde hair stood out against the dark blue curtains.

'It will be a quick sprint back to the hall tonight,' said Wren.

Freya snapped out of her near trance and looked over at Wren. 'Yes, it will be,' said Freya quietly.

Wren leaned over to Freya and said in a near whisper, 'Jinx doesn't like me. I can understand why. I was *beastly* to her and most everyone at the Rhodesia Club. I regret it. I don't know what comes over me sometimes.'

'Jinx will give you another chance. She's really nice. And you are nice, under all of that armour,' said Freya, and she smiled.

Wren smiled. She didn't know what to say. She decided not to respond. Yes, Freya was right. Wren's imperiousness was her armour. It had protected her throughout her childhood and at her posh boarding school. It had kept people at a distance needed to protect her secrets and herself. It wouldn't be easy to shed it now. The confrontation with Freya that night after the Formal Hall had been pivotal. Wren wanted friends, but she didn't want her true situation known. Her family's relative poverty was humiliating for her. A lot of people were having a hard time, but Wren was a feudal lord. Well, she was supposed to be. That meant she had to protect the village, the castle, and the house. But without money or resources, how could she?

'Ginza was *marvellous*,' said Jinx in her Sloane intonation. 'I have never seen anything like it. The fashion show was unbelievable. I was scared, but the other girls were really nice. There was a really sweet Austrian model. She must have been six feet tall and blonde. She had the most beautiful blue eyes, like Freya's. She could see I was nervous, and just before the fashion show began, she took me aside and talked with me. She told me that I should just look straight ahead and pretend the crowd wasn't there. She said, "Pick a point on the wall ahead of you and try to focus on it; that will help you deal with your nervousness." She was right. I did just that, and it worked,' said Jinx and she smiled. 'The fashion show is online, on the company website. It's already been watched millions of times.'

Suga smiled and said impishly, 'Did you model only bikinis, Jinx?'

Jinx blushed. So did Bram—which Jinx found endearing.

Suga took her smartphone out of her pocket and started to tap on it. 'Shall we have a look?'

Jinx blushed again, but said nothing. She wanted Rex to see the show. Jinx wanted Rex to see her in a bikini. Jinx turned slightly and looked at Rex. He was blushing. He noticed Jinx and looked away. Jinx smiled.

'Let me see too,' said Pasha, who appeared out of no where.

THE FASHION SHOW IN TOKYO

The fashion show began on the relatively large screen of Suga's cell phone. The cavernous room in Ginza was filled to capacity. The catwalk had been constructed over a long, narrow pool of water. The first model to appear was Jinx. She was wearing a white bikini. Her glossy black hair, cut into a razor-sharp chin length bob, shimmered in the lights from the narrow pool and the stage lights which followed each girl as they made their way down the runway. Jinx was stunningly beautiful. Her body was athletic (years of horseback riding and working on the family farm had left Jinx toned) and lithe. She moved like a panther. One of the American models had shown her how to do it. Freya walked like that naturally; for Jinx, it was a skill she had to quickly acquire—and she did just that. The lights in the pool reflected the ripples in the clear water onto the models as they walked down the catwalk. When Jinx made her way down the runway, the audience clapped and a loud murmuring could be heard over the thumping music. When Jinx reached the end of the catwalk, she paused for just a second, and then turned, exposing every curve of her teenage body.

The audience came alive, as if it were one being. Jinx walked back down the catwalk and then stepped down behind the stage. She quickly changed into a white one-piece swimsuit and then was hurriedly led back to the steps leading up to the catwalk by one of the fashion assistants. Jinx noticed the head designer just before she climbed the steps; the middle-aged Japanese woman was clapping and smiling. Jinx felt a wave of energy and confidence surge through her. She ascended the steps and stepped out onto the catwalk. The audience collectively turned as one to look at Jinx, the new undoubted 'It Girl' of Japan. Jinx chose a point ahead of her and started walking. The high heels hurt, but they did wonders for her posture. Jinx walked down the catwalk, energy surged through her and seem to flow into the audience. The atmosphere was electric; a wave of the fantastic swept over the crowd and energized everyone in the room. The cavernous hall exploded with applause. Jinx fed off of the audience and they fed off of her. Jinx was elated. Jinx stopped at the end of the catwalk—okay, Jinx, now turn—but that didn't happen as it was supposed to. Jinx stopped and before turning stoney faced like an automaton, Jinx paused for a second and smiled seductively, something she had never done before. It seemed to come so naturally. The audience roared with approval.

Jinx turned and then began her walk back down the catwalk past the other models. Jinx wasn't there anymore; she was flying somewhere else. Her mind seemed to leave her body. Jinx couldn't believe it. She was in Tokyo, Japan and walking the catwalk. Picked out of obscurity; a teenage girl that had never thought of herself as that attractive, let alone beautiful. And yet, here she was. The world was now full of possibilities. Jinx's future was limitless.

Jinx made her way down the steps and backstage. When she stepped off the last step, Jinx looked around. The assistants were slack jawed; the other models were clapping and smiling. Jinx was stunned. Fifteen minutes earlier, she was just another teenager from a small village in Surrey, and now Jinx was The Goddess of Ginza.

'They love you, Jinx!' said the young and beautiful Austrian model in a white bikini.

'Ok, now, quickly!' said the young Japanese woman. Jinx pulled the white one piece suit off and stepped naked out of it. With the help of the assistant, she put on the silver bikini. In less than thirty seconds Jinx was ascending the steps to the catwalk once more. Jinx, glittering in the metallic silver bikini, appeared at the end of the catwalk. The lights moved and pulsed with the music; one lone spot light suddenly shone exclusively on her. Jinx moved forward; the audience burst into applause. The music thumped and the audience followed her every step and movement. Jinx, resplendent in a barely there bikini, no longer needed to pick a point and stare; she was pure confidence.

Jinx reached the end of the catwalk, paused, and then slowly turned. The audience applauded wildly, the volume of their clapping and cheering increased as she executed the turn at the end of the runway. She walked back and at the end of the catwalk she could see the head designer clapping surrounded by the other bikini clad models. Jinx made her way to the end of the catwalk and then stopped, turned, and as choreographed earlier, stood next to the head designer.

A bluish white beam of light then illuminated the fashion designer and the models on the stage in a sudden burst of light. The audience stood and cheered and clapped. The head designer took a few steps forward, bowed in three directions, and then exited the stage followed by the other models. The show was over, but the audience continued to clap and shout.

The show had been successful beyond the wildest dreams of the designer, the CEO, and the shareholders. And Jinx.

SNOWFALL
At ten minutes to eleven, the girls put their shoes on and walked down the wooden staircase and left the men's residence hall through the large wooden double doors. The snow was still falling and the run through the ankle deep snow had been freezing and exhilarating for everyone, especially Jinx. She had never seen video of the show; the images on the screen had been a revelation. Jinx was now a supermodel—at least in Japan. And Jinx had noticed the awed silence that followed the video of the fashion show. Everyone in the room looked at Jinx in an entirely different light now. And Jinx suddenly felt different. She was confident and now had razor sharp direction: she would declare her love for Rex, he would (undoubtably) declare his love for her; they would become engaged and marry the Saturday after graduation. They would have children and live in a house in Surrey near her family. They would act on stage and in film, and they would both be happy.

Jinx had been so caught up in the night's events that she had forgot to tell them that she had won the award for Best Actress at the film festival in Tokyo and that the independent film she had starred in had won the Audience Prize.

BRAMWELL

The get together the night before had been brief, but Bram had met a lot of really nice people, mostly theatre people. They were exciting and different. And the girls in the Drama Club were really attractive and interesting. Bramwell wished that he could act; he would join the Drama Club.

Bramwell returned to his dorm room on the first floor of the residence hall. He lived alone. Not by choice. The room assignments for new students were random. He had been assigned one of the small rooms with a window onto the grass quad. Bram liked his room. Bram had decorated the white walls with a flag of St George and a few photos from home. His single bed had white cotton sheets (embroidered with his family's coat of arms on one corner in blue thread) and grey wool blankets edged in blue. Hanging from a wooden peg next to the wooden wardrobe was a Border Tartan scarf—a gift from his father.

The blond and blue-eyed Bram was attractive, even handsome. His natural shyness had deterred most girls from approaching him. Bram was also a serious student. Most of the girls he had met were not interested in living on a farm. They wanted to move to London and have a career in advertising or fashion. London, for Bram, held little interest. His mother's family lived there, and he would sometimes visit. The small, modest, Edwardian semi-detached where his mother had grown up bordered a park. It was a pleasant area, but London itself no longer was. Even his mother rarely visited. No, Northumberland was where Bram's heart was. Did Suga like him? Bram doubted it, but he was only nineteen and the world hadn't disappointed him that much yet. Bram was optimistic.

Gemma—The Carthage Option—Another Lost Weekend

THE MIDLANDS

The fire had gone out sometime in the early hours of the morning. While Suga and Pasha, warmed by two room heaters, had remained warm under a duvet and wool blankets. Freya, Jinx, and Wren had not. The three teenage undergraduates, lying on thin mattresses and enveloped in white cotton sheets, under white duvets, and white pillows, had been stirred awake by the drop in temperature.

Freya sat up in bed and looked out the white sash windows. The snow had stopped. Outside the grass quad, empty plinth, and ornate stone buildings were covered in snow; an ocean of white under clear blue skies. Freya suddenly shuddered involuntarily. It was cold. Not freezing cold, but cold. Freya laid back down and covered herself with her white duvet.

Freya looked up at the white plaster ceiling. This afternoon there would be another dress rehearsal; this time Jinx would participate. Jinx. Amazing. Jinx had done it. She was successful. Freya wasn't jealous. She was happy for her. Freya wondered how much money she had made from the fashion show. Had Jinx signed a modelling contract with the swimwear company? Freya hoped she had. Freya hoped the contract would pay a lot. The swimwear brand was only a few years old and neither large nor well known. Well, that is until last week. Yes, Jinx would be in demand.

'What time is it,' said Jinx sleepily. She then pulled the wool blankets up around her.

Freya looked at the clock on the mantlepiece (she wasn't about to get out of bed and look at her wrist watch that was lying on Suga's desk). 'It's 7:29.'

Jinx covered her mouth and yawned. 'Any weekend plans, Freya?'

'How about we visit my house in Mercia? It's only an hour away if we take the train. The station is at the edge of the village. I could call my mother and have her pick us up?' said Wren. No one had even realized that she was awake. She was sleeping on the other side of Freya.

Freya looked the other direction. Wren, her long, glossy honey blonde hair was loose and her bangs partially covered her blue eyes. Yes, she was as strikingly beautiful as Jinx, only different. Wren smiled.

'Are you sure? Shouldn't you telephone and ask your mother first?' asked Freya.

'Mother wrote and invited me to bring home friends one weekend,' said

Wren happily. 'The roof has been repaired and the interior repainted. Electricity and running water are limited, but the house is warm in the winter. I can show you around the castle ruins. They are not open for tours, so it would be a real exclusive.'

Freya looked over at Jinx. Jinx smiled. 'I haven't visited a castle, ruined or otherwise in *yonks*,' said Jinx.

Freya smiled. 'Alright. After rehearsal we can board the train.'

'Let's invite Wallace, Suga, and Pasha too,' said Wren excitedly.

'Pasha's taking the train to London to meet her parents this weekend. And Suga is going to visit her family in Scotland. I don't know what Wallis is up to,' said Freya sleepily.

'I'll text her right now and ask,' said Wren.

'I need to take a shower before class,' said Jinx.

'Oh, that. Well, the furnace is still out, so there is no hot water. Unless you boil it yourself. Or unless you like ice cold showers,' said Freya.

'I'm used to them,' said Wren. 'The furnace goes out all the time at home.'

'Is it out now?' asked Freya.

Wren smiled. 'We'll find out.'

THE BRISTOL MOTORCAR

Wallis had been thrilled by the offer to visit Wren's family pile; after all, Wren's family was an ancient one and Wren's family still lived on their ancestral lands. And Wren was a fellow Hon and future baroness by Writ, like Wallis.

Wallis preferred to drive everyone to Wren's village in her mother's grey 1966 Bristol Mark II motorcar. Wallis loved the Bristol. It had been purchased by her grandfather from the showroom in Kensington brand new. It was the family car. Wallis would never sell it. Her mother preferred to drive her white VW Polo around Surrey, so Wallis had asked to drive it to Muddy Hills. The 11th Baroness had agreed. Best the car be driven than allowed to rust to pieces in the garage.

'Can you drive in snow?' asked Jinx.

'Of course. Mummy taught me. And besides, how bad could the snow be?' replied Wallis.

THE RHODES THEATRE
Jinx's appearance on stage that afternoon created quite the stir. Freshly arrived from Tokyo, Jinx had an aura of glamor around her that was electric. Jinx had always been attractive, but now she was imbued with a beauty that bordered on the supernatural. How was it that so few had noticed for so long?

Jinx's scene with Rex was deeply emotional; the chemistry between them was palpable; the only question was who was more magnetic: Jinx or Rex?

The final confrontation between Freya and Jinx (Cleopatra and Arsinoë) had been amazing; the two actresses, as close as sisters, portrayed their characters as deeply wounded by each other's betrayal. And, amazingly, Jinx had outshone Freya. It was Jinx whose beauty had eclipsed Freya's.

'Farewell, sister.'

If there was a dry eye in the theatre, it didn't belong to Elfie, the young director.

As the final curtain descended, the cast burst into spontaneous applause.

THE RESIDENCE HALL
The battered leather box suitcase sat open on the bed. Jinx had packed a pair of faded blue jeans, and a pair of dark khaki wool trousers, two white cotton blouses, and several other things which she couldn't remember into

the suitcase. She wore a beige v-neck sweater, a white cotton blouse, and a pair of blue wool trousers.

Jinx wrapped the dark blue and white wool scarf of her all-girl boarding school in Wales around her neck and shoulders. While not very old (founded in 1954) or prestigious as All Saints (it was third tier), the small school was still an excellent school. Freya always wore her All Saints scarf, even though she had really had a difficult time there, so why shouldn't Jinx who had had an uneven, if not all together unpleasant time there, wear hers?

It was freezing cold in Jinx's room. She had only returned to pack. Freya had packed her suitcase that morning. Her leather suitcase sat on the bed. Freya was not there. She was most likely in Wallis' warm alcove room. Jinx could see her breath materialize in the cold room. It was a miracle the pipes had not frozen and burst.

Suddenly there was a commotion next door and Jinx could hear shouting. Jinx opened the door to her room and looked outside. Two young South Korean girls exited the room that was next door to Jinx's and water followed them out into the hall.

Jinx had spoken (or thought) too soon. Jinx met the two soaked students in the hallway; cold water swirled around them. They were standing in an icy stream.

'The pipes in the ceiling have burst!' said Nara, one of the panicked young Korean undergraduates.

'Let's get your things out of your room,' said Jinx. 'I'll help you bring them into my room.'

'Thank you, Jinx!' said the other Korean undergraduate.

Jinx ran into the room and found herself splashing through the water and trying to avoid the water that was pouring from the ceiling. Jinx helped the girls carry whatever she could into her own room next door. A moment later Elfie appeared and joined them. Another young Rhodesian walked down the hall and took out her smartphone. She telephoned the physical plant.

Fortunately for the young Korean girls next door, the water had been turned off days before and the amount of water which spilled from the ceiling had been limited. Still, the room was soaked.

Jinx and Freya's room was soon filled with wet clothes hanging from makeshift clothes lines and plastic bins and cardboard boxes of textbooks and belongings. It wasn't that much, really. Few of the students kept much in their rooms beyond a suitcase or two of clothing and their books. And the Korean girls had managed to save their black academic robes from getting ruined. They now hung in Jinx's wardrobe.

The entire episode had lasted only fifteen minutes. The dorm room had been emptied and two middle-aged men, in dark blue overalls, arrived from the physical plant to access the damage. The room was flooded and had been left unlivable. Repairs would begin immediately.

Elfie invited the two undergraduates to stay in her large room with her roommate (a Welsh girl from Carmarthen). Nara, the taller of the two Korean undergraduates, was acting in The Ptolemies and was a friend of Elfie's. Nara played one of Arsinoë's courtiers. The attractive teenage Nara's ambition was to become a flight attendant. Nara had an edge to her personality that Jinx liked. Jinx told the girls that they could keep their belongings in her room for as long as necessary.

'Thank you, Jinx. You are really nice,' said Nara.

Freya and Wallis appeared in Freya's and Jinx's room a half an hour after the pipes had burst.

'I do hope the girls managed to get everything out before their clothes and books were ruined,' said Wallis.

'Yes, fortunately, their books and papers were kept in a book shelf near the door. Their clothes got soaked, but they will dry,' said Jinx as she stood in her room crisscrossed with clotheslines and damp clothing.

Freya surveyed the scene. 'We should probably ask for a room heater to help dry their clothes; otherwise, the wet clothes will freeze in the room and won't dry until spring.'

THE ROAD TO MERCIA

The Bristol Mark II glided down the country road. The roads had been cleared earlier in the day and were easy to navigate. Wallis drove carefully. The fields on either side of the road were white blankets of snow for as far as their young and healthy eyes could see. Freya and Wren sat in the back seat while Jinx sat in the front next to Wallis. The white landscape met the blue skies somewhere. Yes, the countryside was beautiful—still beautiful—they hadn't managed to ruin that yet, not yet.

'Mummy had the car upgraded by Bristol a few years ago. Modern seat belts, a new leather interior, and even a new engine and automatic transmission. She had the car repainted too. I wanted dark blue, but Mummy insisted on keeping it the original grey. The red leather interior was the original color too. I wanted black or beige.'

'I think it's beautiful,' said Jinx happily.

'Thank you. Yes, I love the car. And I think Mummy was right. It's best to keep the original color and interior. It's how Grandfather wanted it.'

As the car neared the village, the fiery Sun began its descent. It wasn't even four o'clock, and the winter was reclaiming the day. The Bristol Mark II slowed as it approached a heavily wooded and snow covered turn off. 'Yes, just ahead is the road to the village, Wren said excitedly. It was already noticeably darker.

'There is a village nearby?' asked Wallis.

'Yes, it is completely hidden behind the forest. We own the land on either side of the road. We haven't allowed any of the trees to be cut down since the Restoration. My house is located a hundred yards down the road and on the right,' said Wren.

Wallis turned on the headlights; the orange rays of twilight flickered over the car as it motored slowly down the country road through the thick forest. And there, on the right, barely visible behind the tall, ancient trees, just as Wren had said, was the family pile. Wallis decelerated, used the turn signal, and slowly turned onto the long snow-covered road and drove through the stone Jacobean gates. She rolled to a gentle stop and then turned off the engine.

Outside, the Grade I listed two-storey stone house loomed up before them. Its stone walls were illuminated in the fiery orange light of twilight, an optical effect magnified by the light reflected off of the snow.

THE FAMILY PILE

Wren's manor house was an irregular, two-storey grey stone building. The original fortified medieval manor house was badly damaged in the English Civil War. When the family returned from exile, they didn't have enough money to restore the house completely, so the reconstruction of the manor house had taken place over centuries. Sections of the house were reconstructed or completely rebuilt when the family could afford to do it. The entrance to the house was a set of large, wooden, Jacobean double doors that had been installed in 1661. Though heavily weathered, the entrance was still quite imposing. The great hall of the Medieval manor house had been destroyed in the English Civil War. When the house was restored after the Restoration in 1660, the family had the former great hall rebuilt as a drawing room with a Jacobean plaster ceiling and a large ornate marble fireplace. If one looked carefully at the house, one could see where the dry ashlar stone masonry ended and the Portland stone began. The house had been partially rebuilt in the late 1600s with sash windows. The stone house, an eclectic mixture of Medieval, Tudor, Jacobean, Georgian, Victorian, and Edwardian architecture should not have worked, but it did. The house had come together seamlessly and was hauntingly beautiful.

The double doors opened and Wren's parents, both in country tweeds, stepped out onto the stone landing. Wren's father was blond and stood ramrod straight. He was a retired army major; he had lost none of his military bearing. Wren's mother had honey blonde hair and blue eyes. Wren bore a strong resemblance to her. Both her parents were attractive and looked much younger than Freya had expected they would. (They were only in their mid-forties, but both looked several years younger.)

Wren smiled. It was obvious that she really loved her parents and was happy to see them again.

The girls all got out of the grey automobile. Bathed in the dying orange light of twilight, they all made their way up the stone steps of the manor house, snow crunching underfoot. Wren's parents met them at the top of the steps.

'Welcome to our home,' said the 23rd Baron in a posh and almost Sloaney intonation. The baron's blonde hair had been cut like a British army officer's. Dressed in a grey overcheck twill tweed jacket, white dress shirt, and dark grey wool trousers, the baron looked more like a movie star, than a retired career army officer. The baron's jaw looked like it had been chiseled out of marble. He had the profile of a Roman god—or perhaps just a statue of one. Perhaps Wren had inherited her looks from her youthful and handsome father? Wren's mother, the baroness, was slender and had a clear, youthful, and glowing complexion. She was the epitome of Rhodesian beauty. The way Wren had spoken about her parents at Muddy Hills, Freya had expected to meet two elderly and frail people dressed in rags; not the youthful, attractive, and sharply attired couple that now stood before her.

Wren's teenage guests smiled. It was almost dark and the cold winter air was beginning to be felt.

'Let's head inside, girls. I'll show you to your room,' said Wren's mother in a decidedly Rhodesian accent that made Jinx smile.

The entry hall floor was the traditional black and white tile pattern popular in many great houses—and the not so great. Though cracked in places, the centuries old tiles had maintained their glossiness and were dazzlingly beautiful, in a uniquely English way. The Tudor wood paneling of the room had been replaced long ago. Now stone walls enclosed the entry hall. An almost modern minimalist space had been created. The white walls of the hall had been painted just a week before by Wren's parents. Years of experience gained painting and repainting the house had made them as good as any professional painter. A marble staircase led to the second floor. It had been installed by Wren's family in 1663 and had nearly bankrupted her ancestors, but it had been worth it then and it was worth it now. The stairs were a tribute to the family's indomitability. The entry hall's wall mounted light fixtures had all been repaired and the room was illuminated in soft white light. Yes, the room was beautiful. The walls were not ornate. The floor tiles were still cracked and chipped. The light fixtures unadorned and utilitarian. The entry hall was quite plain; however, the house radiated the ancient. This house had belonged in Wren's family for almost a thousand years. It was something about being here—in this place—with this ancient family, that made it all special. Freya and the other girls were impressed.

Wren froze and looked around the entry hall in amazement. She had never seen the house look this opulent. It's amazing what a fresh coat of white paint can do for a room. She looked at her mother standing off to one side and smiled. The baroness smiled back.

Please follow me, girls,' said the baroness as she walked up the marble staircase. The baroness, in a dark blue Harris Tweed skirt, white cotton blouse with open cuffs, a beige v-neck sweater, and a pair of blue suede flats, glided up the stairs. The girls followed Wren's mother up the staircase and down the white walled hallway which still smelt of fresh paint, the hardwood floor creaking with every step, until they reached a wide, glossy white door. The baroness opened it and entered. The girls filed in behind her.

THE BEDROOM
'We haven't used this bedroom in a long time. But, as you can see, there is a large fireplace and room for four beds,' said the baroness in a Rhodesian accent.

The walls also had a fresh coat of white paint on them. On either side of the marble fireplace were standing lamps topped but hand blown glass orbs. They gave off enough light to illuminate most of the room. A smaller lamp on an antique wooden dresser illuminated the rest of the room. The overall effect was rather pleasant. The beds were folding metal camp beds (surplus from The Great War) with brand-new mattresses, white cotton bedding, pillows, and navy blue wool blankets. They had been placed at the end of the room near the fireplace.

Above the fireplace was a gilt framed painting of one Wren's illustrious ancestors who had been killed in the English Civil War. The young man's grieving father had taken the painting with him when he went into exile on the continent during the Interregnum, and then returned with it in 1660. The baron's son had been killed leading a cavalry charge during the war. The young cavalier had been shot off his horse, left badly wounded, and when surrounded by Parliamentarian soldiers, had refused to surrender and been cut down in a hail of bullets. His final words, as recorded by an officer of the New Model Army, had been, 'God save the King.'

'I hope you girls don't mind camping out up here. The food served in the kitchen will more than make up for any discomfort,' said the baroness.

'I love this room,' said Jinx in an unbridled Rhodesian accent.

Wren's mother turned towards Jinx, smiled, and said, 'Do I hear Bulawayo?'

'Yes, my mother is from Bulawayo,' said Jinx happily.

'So am I,' said the baroness.

Jinx had never felt more connected to someone outside of her family. Yes, Wren's mother had been born in Bulawayo, just like Jinx's (Jane's) own mother.

'Dinner will be served at 8pm. I hope you like steak,' said the baroness. And we will also be serving fresh vegetables grown in our green house and tropical fruit from our orangery. Don't worry; I'm a tolerable chef,' said the baroness, and she smiled.

'Steak is my favorite, ma'am,' said Freya politely.

'Yes, nothing like grilled beef, ma'am,' said Wallis in her Sloaney intonation.

'Let's go downstairs and get your luggage before it starts to snow again,' said the baroness.

'Please let us do that, ma'am. We can bring up our own luggage. We don't have that much,' said Wallis.

'Alright. Then I will leave you girls to it. I'm sure Wren will want to give you a tour. A word of caution, now that the house is undergoing repairs, the ghosts will probably start moving back in. It's best if you tour the house in the daytime,' said the baroness mischievously.

Gemma—The Carthage Option—The Warlord

LONDON
He slowly and carefully wrapped the scarf around his neck and shoulders. Then he took it off and rewrapped it around his neck and shoulders again. He looked at his reflection in the mirror. Yes, his once brown hair was turning silver and grey—just like his mother's had turned before her life had ended. He stared at his reflection in the mirror. He turned his head to one side, and then the other. Yes, he resembled his mother. He also shared some of her facial expressions. He hadn't noticed that until one day he had caught his reflection in the windows of a store front one afternoon while talking quietly on his cell phone. He froze when he saw his mother's face staring back at him in the glass. He stopped talking to the client on the phone.

He had almost forgotten what his mother's face had looked like. He had escaped without anything but the clothes on his back. Not true. He had carried with him one thing: a paper card that his mother had sent to him years before. She had written him a short note in her beautiful handwriting. She had written that she loved him. He had kept this fragile piece of thin carboard (or was it thick paper?) with him as he retreated with the others. He had wrapped it in a piece of wax paper to protect it and carried it in one of the pockets of his BDUs. This card had become his most valued possession. It was the only proof he had that his mother had once existed.

His mother had been brutalized and murdered. Her body had been piled up in a house in the center of the village with the lifeless bodies of her neighbors and burned to charred bones and ashes by **evil creatures** that some people still called 'humans'. But the Revenant knew better. These evil creatures knew better too.

One day, he promised himself, he would find these evil creatures. And he would kill every single one of them. Slowly. He knew who they were. He would find them. When the time came, he would know where to look.

If he could secure Carter Holland's new country, then he would have nearly unlimited resources to avenge his family, his friends, and his people. Carter Holland was expecting a lot of him, but Carter Holland richly rewarded those who were loyal to him. It was through this new country that the Revenant would have the ability—the power—to do anything he wanted. The army would be his army. The air force and the navy too. The ranks of Carter Holland's military would be filled with thousands of useless locals who were only there to collect a paycheck. The core of the new armed forces would be a different story. The Revenant had put together an army of hardened men like himself. They were loyal to the Revenant. And they would follow his orders without question. Not out of blind obedience, but because they all desired the same things. Eventually the Revenant would go home with his new army and reconquer his homeland. He would leave Carter alone to rule over his new country. The Revenant had no desire to rule anything. He only wanted revenge. So did those at the core of the Revenant's new army. And they would have it. **Carter Holland would be the way.**

THE NECROPOLIS RAILWAY STATION
The three-storey building had a façade of Portland stone. The opulent and large central entrance had been reserved for first class mourners. The second class mourners had entered through a less ornate entrance nearly a

block away. The third class mourners had entered through an austere and functional side entrance.

The station, which had opened in 1854, had been closed in 1923, and never re-opened. The interior was a collection of the ornate, the opulent, and the austere. Which rooms one had found themselves had all depended on how much money the mourners had had. Nothing else really. The bereaved would gather in the station in South London and then board a train that would take them to a cemetery outside of London.

The cemetery had reached capacity in the winter of 1923; The war dead of the Great War had filled most of what space remained. The post-war years had seen it filled with those that the war dead had left behind. The land surrounding the cemetery was in private hands and the owners had all refused to sell any more of it. It was decided to close the station.

THE 1st BARON
The necropolis train station had been purchased by a wealthy industrialist in 1924 who had planned to turn it into a private railway station. It was from here that he would board his ostentatious private train and steam towards the thousand acres of land outside of London which surrounded the Georgian country house that had once belonged to an ancient noble family.

THE 11th BARON
The war had seen the 11th Baron's only child, a twenty-one-year-old son, killed in 1916, thus leaving the widower without an heir and alone. Bankrupted by the total loss of the family fortune he had invested in Czarist Russia before the war and which had been subsequently expropriated by the Bolsheviks in Russia in 1917, the old man, completely broken, gave up and sold the house to the upstart 1st Baron in 1919.

The 11th Baron, a cavalry officer who had been highly decorated for bravery in the Battle of Omdurman in the course of the reconquest of the Sudan, the Boer War, and World War One, died a week later, worn out at only 51, another victim of modernity (or was that progress?) The newly created 1st Baron had referred to the entire episode as 'creative destruction.'

That the train would have to pass through mile upon mile of graveyard did not trouble the 1st Baron in the slightest.

It was in his armament factories during the First World War that he had made his fortune. The war profiteer had been elevated into the House of Lords. A new barony had been created. His three sons, all able-bodied young men, had avoided military service; they had been 'needed on the 'Home Front' to help their father manage the factories. The three profligate offspring of the 1st Baron only set foot in one of the factories when Members of Parliament or a government minister toured one of the facilities. The three 'Honourables' had spent the war hosting luncheons and parities at London's poshest hotels and restaurants. Too many questions were being asked in parliament about the boys, so the 1st Baron quietly arranged for them to receive army commissions in 1917 and serve in various regimental staff positions—none saw combat, but all would go on to be decorated, the oldest son with a D.S.O. (for exactly what remained a mystery, even to the future 2nd Baron). The final days of the war saw all three young 'Hons' wintering in Monaco.

The Cosmos, however, requires balance.

In 1923, the three 'Hons' were seen by a group of 'Bright Young Things' at ten minutes past midnight racing down a cobblestone street in London in two open top automobiles in the company of three teenage chorus girls. A moment later a loud crash was heard and all three sons and the chorus girls were dead. The dissolute 'Hons' had died unmourned, except by their father. The 1st Baron had been left broken by their deaths. The scandal that followed had seen the sordid details of their lives revealed in the press, along with their avoidance of front line military service. The 1st Baron retreated to his country house and never left. He died in 1930 bankrupted by the stock market crash of 1929.

The baronial title went extinct upon his death.

The train station was sold to someone who sold it to someone else who passed away before he could do anything with it.

Today it was owned by Carter Holland.

This winter night found it the meeting place of a group of unusual men.

A svelte man pointed to the glowing screen of a silver cased laptop computer which had been place atop an old wooden desk. Occasionally he would tap on the keyboard and a photo would appear on the glowing screen or a film clip would play as he spoke. All four men watched the screen in rapt attention.

'At 5:17am the subject, wearing a dark blue hooded parka and thick black framed glasses, left the semi-detached in Corbridge.'

'Where's Corbridge?' asked the Revenant, his face partially lit in shadow.

'It's a small village in Northumberland,' replied the svelte, middle-aged man.

'Alright. Please continue.'

'The subject walked to St Andrews church. He entered. We didn't follow him. That would have given away the game and led to a confrontation. We waited. Five minutes later a middle-aged man in a dark blue parka, with the hood up, and a young woman in a dark grey jumper and a large scarf wrapped around most of her face, entered the church together. Both were wearing eyeglasses. We haven't yet identified either of them.

'Did you try facial recognition?'

'Yes. They aren't in the system; which seems highly unlikely. Considering the effectiveness of the system, we can only assume they were wearing some kind of disguise to disrupt the imaging software. We believe the eyeglasses they were all wearing disrupt facial recognition as well. Also, their faces were partially covered and it was still dark. The sun hadn't risen yet.'

'Okay. Then what happened? asked the Revenant quietly.

We waited outside for exactly twenty-two minutes. The middle-aged man and young woman left the church. The subject left at some point, but through a different exit.'

'You didn't have men positioned around the church?'

'I did. I believe the subject left via a Saxon Era tunnel to an adjoining building. But we aren't sure.'

'Then he detected your presence?'

'Yes. Or the others did,' said the man in French accented English. (Though French was not his native language; he had served in the French Foreign Legion. The svelte man had been born faraway from France.)

The Revenant crossed his arms and looked at the man speaking to him. The man was middle-aged, slender, and had dark hair. He carried himself with noticeable military bearing. The man wore faded blue jeans, and black wool jumper, and a dark grey wool scarf. The man wore a German dive watch secured to his wrist with a black rubber strap. The Revenant had known him for almost two decades. He was a loyal, brave, and highly competent soldier. If the subject had managed to shake him, it was a reflection of the subject's own abilities, rather than the abilities of the man standing before him.

'Who owns the house in Corbridge?' asked the Revenant.

'A real estate development company based in Manchester. No known connection to Enoch Tara or the subject. It is listed as a short term rental online. The renter undoubtably used a fake name.'

'Now they know they are being spied upon,' said the Revenant.

'I doubt this is new to them.'

'Probably not. That's why they are meeting in obscure places and using fake names and masking their identities,' replied the Revenant.

The men were meeting in an unheated and disused office on the first floor of the unheated and disused necropolis train station in London. The office was windowless; the only natural light came from a glass transom window above the office door. The office walls were of polished Circassian walnut. Now the walls were covered in dust and cobwebs. The office itself had a large wooden desk and four wooden chairs. A single, modern, battery powered lantern which had been placed on the desk, illuminated the room in a pale, somber light. The four men in the office were all standing. Carter Holland paid for routine maintenance and for the station (including the offices) to be thoroughly cleaned three times a year. It had been almost four months since the crews had been through the station. It showed.

The Revenant turned to a different man who was dressed in a pair of grey wool trousers, a blue dress shirt, a dark blue silk necktie, and a dark grey overcoat. He looked like a City banker. He wasn't one.

'What have you learned?' asked the Revenant in his indeterminable accent.

'That Enoch Tara sometimes travels alone. Without any security. He still does. I can't believe it.'

'Why is that?' asked the Revenant.

'I really don't know. Tara is a risktaker. Perhaps going without security sometimes is a component of his personality?' replied the man in the dark grey overcoat.

'When is Tara usually alone?' asked the Revenant.

'There is no regular schedule. He always has security at the house in Marble Arch, at least on the first floor and security teams three blocks out. The bank in the City has a separate security team. A security team is always there. There is a caretaker on the island in Scotland. He is armed. He is a retired submariner from the Royal Navy. When Tara is driven around London, security is around him,' said the man quietly; his accented English had become more noticeably foreign the longer he talked to the Revenant.

'When is Tara usually alone?' asked the Revenant.

'When he is with Gemma Ripley.'

Gemma—The Carthage Option—The Apparitions

MERICA

The baron and baroness hosted the girls in the large medieval kitchen. Surrounded by ancient grey stone walls, a large fireplace, several butcherblock topped counters and a silver SMEG refrigerator. The standard sized appliance looked tiny when compared to the vastness of the kitchen. In the center was a large wooden table and ten high back wooden chairs. There was a Blenheim cast iron stove (circa 1910) and a stainless steel sink that had been installed in the 1950s.

Dinner had been served on inexpensive white porcelain plates and glassware and stainless steel silverware. White cloth napkins had been carefully folded and left on each plate. Sterling silver trays, ladles, bowls, and a teapot had been polished and used at dinner. What little sterling silver the family had left would make an appearance tonight at dinner.

Wren's mother made dinner while Wren's father had carefully set the table. Wren's parents wanted to make a good impression on their daughter's friends. Wren had had a difficult time at her posh boarding school. Wren had written such terribly sad letters home from school about how humiliating it was for her to be around the posh and moneyed students at her all-girl boarding school. How well dressed her classmates were and how Wren had had to conceal virtually every aspect of her life from her spoiled classmates. Wren couldn't afford to have close friends at her boarding school—financially or socially. It had all taken a toll on her. But suddenly, a little over a week ago, Wren had telephoned her mother and told her how she had made friends with some of the girls at Midlands-Hasegawa. Wren had started crying towards the end of the phone call. Something had happened, Wren wouldn't say what, but whatever it was, it had allowed Wren to trust others and realize that there was more to life than money. Wren had found friends who understood her—apparently. Wren's parents were happy, really happy. They had only ever wanted for Wren, their only child, to be happy. And now she was. That's all that really mattered.

The baroness sent her daughter a text message when dinner was ready. The girls changed into wool trousers and knitted jumpers. It was a question of warmth. When the girls left the bedroom, Wren was careful to extinguish the fire in the fireplace. The furnace wasn't working that well at the moment; the best way to heat the rooms were the fireplaces.

'Yes, life here is medieval,' said Wren happily as the girls walked down the cold hallway and made their way down the marble staircase.

Dinner was fantastic. Grilled beef, fresh steamed vegetables, brown rice, and freshly picked tropical fruit from the Edwardian orangery.

'It's nice to have all of you here,' said the baron. 'What are you planning to do this weekend?'

'I thought I would show everyone around the village tomorrow and then take them on a tour of the castle,' said Wren.

'Dress warmly, girls. It's freezing in the castle in the winter,' said the baroness.

'Wren told me how the Roundheads had destroyed the castle during the Civil War, sir. *How beastly.* They did the same to my family's castle in Surrey,' said Wallis in her Sloaney intonation.

The 23rd Baron shook his head. 'Yes, the Civil War inflicted wounds on the family that have never healed.'

'My family lost three of our ancestors at the Battle of Marston Moor,' said Freya.

'We lost one of the family at the Battle of Longport,' said Wallis.

'I don't know how many of my family were lost, but my mother told me that we had supported the King,' said Jinx in her unique Rhodesian Sloane

Ranger intonation.

'To the King,' said Wren as she stood with a glass of water.

Everyone stood and toasted the martyred King Charles I.

'To the King.'

'To the Queen,' said the baron solemnly.

'To the Queen,' said everyone around the table. (Well, everyone but Jinx, who simply held up her glass and said 'to the Crown' under her breath.)

THE UPSTAIRS BEDROOM
'Is the house really haunted?' asked Jinx.

'Supposedly. I mean, that's what everyone says,' replied Wren. Wren was wearing a pair of dark blue pyjama bottoms (with white piping), a pair of blue velvet slippers, and an old beige knit sweater with several holes in it. Wren was rearranging the logs in the fireplace with a wrought iron fire poker. The fire poker was well over a hundred and fifty years old. It had been made by the village blacksmith and was engraved with the family's coat of arms on the handle. 'There are said to be ghosts in every room of the house.'

Jinx, clad in a pair of pale blue flannel pyjama bottoms and a dark blue hoodie, was already under the covers of her fold out surplus army camp bed. 'What do you mean? Every room? Even this room?' Jinx looked around the large bedroom nervously.

'Yes. But don't worry. I've never seen one,' said Wren as she poked at the glowing orange embers in the fireplace.

'What ghost lives in this room,' asked Wallis.

'Do you have any iron horse shoes in here?' aske Freya.

'No,' said Wren and she continued to poke and stir the embers and burning logs. 'Besides, they won't ward off a ghost.'

'What does ward off ghosts?' asked Jinx.

'Nothing,' said Wren as she leaned the wrought iron fire poker against the stone wall of the bedroom.

'So what will we do if a ghost appears in here this weekend?' asked Freya.

'I wouldn't worry too much about it, Freya. I've never seen one.'

Jinx looked outside. 'It's snowing.'

The girls all looked in the directions of the three sash windows at the end of the room. Wallis, in set of red, lavender, and light grey tartan pyjamas (with a rounded collar) and white slippers, walked over to the windows and looked outside. Yes, it was coming down steadily. Wallis noticed that her automobile, partially illuminated by one of the outside lights, was already covered in a thin layer of snow.

'We might to dig the car out of the snow tomorrow, if this keeps up,' said Wallis, and she smiled.

'If the ghosts don't get us first,' said Jinx.

Freya arched an eyebrow.

'Iron horseshoes won't protect us this time,' said Jinx.

'Oh, no you don't, Jinx,' said Freya laughingly.

'What do you mean?' asked Wallis.

Wallis' long, silky, tousled blonde hair was worn over one shoulder. Yes, Wallis, was beautiful; a beauty she had inherited from the Welsh side of her family. She was a near carbon copy her Welsh grandmother. And her cousin, Morgan, the future 7th Baron, bore a strong resemblance to Wallis. Wallis, the future English Baroness, was beautiful in the way that only a Welsh girl could be.

'My dear, Northumbrian friend, Louise told us about the Black Annis, a creature that wanders England in search of prey, one night, and we all ended up sleeping with the lights on,' said Freya and she smiled.

Wren smiled and said, 'We call her Black Agatha around here. Yes, she is a scary one, isn't she?'

'Yes. She is. I telephoned my parents and asked them to mail a horseshoe to Muddy Hills to protect me and Freya,' said Jinx.

'Thank you, Jinx. Very kind,' said Freya.

'We have a ghost that is even more terrifying than the Black Agatha living in the library downstairs,' said Wren quietly.

'Okay. Stop,' said Freya laughingly. 'I am not going through this again.'

'What ghost? There is a ghost downstairs?' asked the nineteen-year-old Wallis.

'Yes,' said Wren.

'Okay, well, you can go downstairs and without me. It is eleven minutes till midnight,' said Freya while looking at the antique clock on the mantlepiece. 'Isn't that when supernatural creatures are at their strongest?' asked Freya.

'Ghosts are always at their strongest,' said Wren.

Freya arched an eyebrow and said, 'I thought you didn't believe in ghosts?'

'I do believe in them. I said I had just never seen one before. I believe in all manner of the supernatural,' said Wren.

'I do too,' said Freya. 'That's why I think we should visit the library in the daytime.'

'No, it's best to visit at night, Freya. It's easier to see apparitions at night,' said Wallis.

'You can go, but I'll stay here,' said Freya.

'Alright, Freya. But, please, don't look in the mirror in the corner while we are away,' said Wren quietly.

Freya burst out laughing. 'Okay, I'll go with you. I don't want to be here alone when the ghost in the mirror drags me into it, never to be seen again.'

The girls all started laughing.

'Is there really a ghost in the mirror?' asked Wallis.

THE LIBRARY
The girls, still in pyjamas, dressed warmly for their nocturnal visit to the library. (Wren had warned them that that part of the house was unheated.) Freya put on her blue quilted jacket; Jinx her beige v-neck sweater and blue and white school scarf; Wallis her dark blue wool jumper. Wren led the way down the marble staircase holding a flashlight.

The entry hall was only dimly lit by a lone standing lamp in the marble tiled hall. The girls walked down a long dark hallway. (The scent of fresh paint filling the corridor.) Wren turned on her torch and a small beam of light illuminated the path ahead. The girls walked to the end of the hall and turned right. Ahead was a set of double doors. Wren held the torch with one hand and turned the clear handmade whirl glass door knob. The glossy white door creaked loudly (of course it did…) when Wren opened it. A blast of icy cold air filled the already cold hallway. A seemingly impenetrable darkness awaited them.

'You first, Wren,' said Freya and she smiled.

'Remember girls, if any apparitions appear, don't worry. They are most likely one of my ancestors. I will speak with them,' said Wren.

Wren stepped into the cold room. The girls filed in after here. The large room beyond was nearly empty. The floor was made up of long, wide planks of (once highly polished) wood. The paneled walls of the library were lined with empty book shelves. The plaster ceiling had suffered a lot of water damage; pieces of plaster littered the floor. In the center of the room were a dozen plastic bins of various sizes filled with books. All of the bins had been carefully sealed. The few remaining ancient books the family still owned, including two illuminated manuscripts from the 13th and 14th centuries, were now kept in a bank vault.

'We sweep up the plaster all the time, but an infinite amount still seems to fall from the ceiling, so the floor is always a mess,' said Wren as the light from her torch swept around the room. 'The ceiling was once really beautiful, but water damage has ruined it. Now that the roof has been fully repaired, we can repair the ceiling of the library. But that will be in the future,' said Wren.

There was a marble fireplace. Freya turned on the lamp on her smartphone and walked across the empty room to get a better look at it. Freya's white slippers made footprints in the white powder dust on the floor. The fireplace was a 19th century English limestone fireplace in the Gothic manner. The jambs and end blocks with quinto acuto arches, the frieze with accompanying arch motifs throughout with a shelf above. It was beautiful in its simplicity.

'That was installed in the 1830s,' said Wren. The girls were now standing in front of the fireplace, which was covered in a light layer of white plaster dust. 'Every year the village chimney sweep carefully cleans all of the fireplaces. I can't wait to have this room restored. I saw photos of it from 1910. It was gorgeous. It's been *yonks* since the library has truly been a library rather than just a place where we store what remains of our book collection.'

This is a nice room,' said Jinx. 'I can imagine what it must have looked like.'

'We have a library in the house in Surrey, but it is much smaller. Actually, the house in Surrey is relatively small. Our library is late Georgian. Quite beautiful,' said Wallis.

'We don't have really have a library. We have books shelves in almost every room of our house in Surrey,' said Jinx. 'One day, I would like you to visit.'

'Yes, I would like that. And you are all invited to my house in Surrey too. Mummy loves to meet my friends. Freya, please do drive your Bristol Fighter. Mummy will feel you a kindred spirit,' said Wallis in posh and Sloaney intonation.

'Father told me that the family once had thousands of books in this library, many of them medieval illuminated manuscripts, but that the Roundheads took most of them when they ransacked the house,' said Wren sadly.

'The house is looking better, I think,' said Freya. 'Soon we will be relaxing in the Jacobean library with you. For sure.'

'I hope so,' said Wren.

'You should see my Welsh cousins' house in Wales. The place is tumbling down around them, but it retains its majesty,' said Wallis. 'You would like my cousin Morgan. He is now a subaltern in the Welsh Guards. It's the family regiment. He read history in university and plans to take over the sheep farm. You would like him, girls; Morgan is truly beautiful,' said Wallis.

'Beautiful like Rex?' asked Wren.

Jinx, standing just behind Wren in the darkness, turned to look at Wren; Jinx's expression was difficult for Freya to make out, but she assumed that Jinx was perhaps jealous. Or more likely nervous, bordering on alarmed. Only Freya knew what Jinx's true feelings for Rex were. Wallis and Wren did not notice Jinx's reaction.

'Yes, like Rex. He is also blonde and svelte. Morgan is a true soldier. But, he will probably enter the reserves when th
 short service commission requirement ends in two years.'

'We speak Welsh when at home in Wales,' said Wallis.

'I can speak Welsh,' said Jinx. 'My boarding school was in Wales and I took Welsh classes there. I also had Welsh roommates. I used to practice speaking it with them.'

Jinx paused for a moment and then said, 'Noswaith dda. Shw mae?'

Wallis smiled. 'I'm fine, and you,' said Wallis laughingly. 'Your pronunciation is flawless, Jinx. It must be the voice training.'

'Thank you, Wallis. I don't speak Welsh perfectly, but I am fairly fluent in it.'

'Is that scarf from your school?' asked Wallis through chattering teeth. Wallis's breath could be seen in the cold air around her.

'Yes. I went to The Borders School. We call the school 'Dress Makers' because the founder was a dress maker. The Honourable Daphne Pennant. Her father, Lord Pennant, the 2nd Baron, and a major-general, had a long career in the British army. He served all over the empire. Their former house is filled with all kinds of things that he collected while in the army, including a stuffed tiger that he killed in India. It was said to be terrorizing the local villages and he hunted down the animal and killed it himself,' said Jinx.

'Is the tiger still on display?' asked Wren.

'Yes, it is,' replied Jinx. 'A group of activists from London showed up last year demanding that we stop serving beef and lamb in the school dining hall to slow climate change and also that we give the stuffed tiger a proper burial. They also said the tiger and other items in the Pennant house symbolized British imperialism and had to be removed and the school should issue a public apology for being founded by Imperialists.'

'Really?' asked Wren.

'Yes. Well, the Pennant family still owns the school, and they called the police, but the police made all kinds of excuses about why they couldn't intervene, even though the activists were trespassing on school property. It was pure chaos. Oh, and they wanted the school to disband the school hunting and animal husbandry clubs because they promoted animal cruelty.'

'What finally happened?' asked Wren.

'Major Pennant, the 3rd Baron, an elderly cousin of the Honourable Daphne Pennant, and the current owner, telephoned the local rugby club, and they chased the protesters away,' said Jinx laughingly.

Jinx crossed her arms and rubbed her arms in an attempt to warm herself.

'The family home is now the school's administrative building. The 'Hon' who founded the school was his only child. She started her own fashion house in London and built a factory in Wales that produced all kinds of clothing, including military uniforms in World War Two. After the war, her business continued to grow and she had three factories, or was it four? She produced wool coats, cotton dresses, wool jumpers, and trousers. She also produced Welsh hats. On special occasions at school we wore black Welsh hats.'

'How big is the school? The family still owns it? Amazing.' asked Wren.

'There are around two hundred students. I'd say half the students are Welsh, almost all of them on partial and full scholarships. There were only a dozen students from England when I was there, most from London. The rest are from Asia and Eastern Europe. The foreign students pay triple the tuition. That's how the school stays afloat financially. The same as Muddy Hills, I suspect. The school is small, but is a good school. I attended on scholarship. Yes, the Pennant family still owns the school. When the 2nd Baron passed away, the school, house, and farm went to his daughter

Daphne. She never married and left everything to her cousin.'

'Were you happy there?' asked Wren.

'Sometimes. Some of the girls were nice. Some of the girls were not. Most of the foreign students were from Korea, Singapore, Japan, and Taiwan. There was a girl from Thailand too. The Chinese Embassy in London banned any mainland Chinese students from attending because the founder's father, the 2nd Baron, had been a member of a British-Taiwan association in the 1950s. The school dormitory was once a uniform factory. All the buildings were once part of a factory complex that made army uniforms and kit. The school's Anglican chapel was once a lorry garage. After the war, the factory closed, and Daphne convinced her father to open a school for the daughters of good Welsh families. She wanted to promote Welsh language and culture. She was also an advocate of girls' education. It was interesting to see Asian girls speaking Welsh. Their families wanted them to become fluent in English, not Welsh. The Asian girls managed to do both. The Pennant family farm is almost a thousand acres. The school sits on ten of them. We have our own dairy cows and a flock of sheep. The students help take care of them. I was in the Hunting, Agricultural, Drama, and Animal Husbandry clubs. I learned a lot from the clubs.'

Where does the family live now?' asked Wren.

'They live in a house a few miles down the road from the school. They still own a dairy too. Major Pennant is *terribly* nice. He still gives speeches in Welsh at school events. It was always fun to see the expressions on the faces of the foreign parents when they attended school events. Mostly Major Pennant runs the family farm.'

'Sounds *rather* pleasant,' said Wren.

'It was alright. I suppose,' said Jinx.

'Any school with a hunting club sounds *absolutely thrilling*,' said Wren in her posh intonation.

'Wren, does your house have any secret doors or tunnels?' asked Wallis. 'You don't have to show them to me, but I am curious.'

Not that I know of.'

'Does your house in Surrey have any secret doors?' asked Freya.

'Yes, a couple,' replied Wallis.

Suddenly a strange creaking came from a darkened corner. The girls all shrieked. They then all turned and looked in the direction of the noise. Wren shone her torch into the corner—nothing but water damaged walls.

'What was that?' asked Jinx.

'Probably just one of my ancestors,' replied Wren.

'That's not funny, Wren,' said Wallis.

'It was probably just the house settling,' said Freya. 'Old houses do that.'

Suddenly there was a loud bang and a cloud of ash and soot swirled out of the fireplace. The girls shrieked once more and then Wren said, 'I think this would be a good time to leave, girls!'

A thunder of slippered feet moved through the darkness with only the violently shaking beam of light from Wren's torch lighting the way. The girls ran out of the room and Wren carefully closed the library doors behind them.

The girls retreated up the stairs and went to bed.

They slept with the lights on.

Gemma—The Carthage Option—The Godparents

THE COUNTRY HOUSE

Violet put on her transparent plastic framed reading glasses and read the instructions printed on the side of the box. Yes, Violet, at forty-one, needed reading glasses. She had worn glasses since she was a teenager, but only as a fashion accessory. Violet had worn frames with clear glass lenses. Now she needed real reading glasses to read anything. Violet was getting older. A year ago, that realization would have distressed and depressed her, but not today. After Violet's profound transformation almost a year ago, Violet accepted aging as inevitable. It was pointless to fret about it. What was important was that she had Freya, Hughie, her parents, her family, and her friends. To be blessed with people who you love and who love you is what truly matters most.

'Poppy? I think we should ask Hector about how to assemble the new pram,' said Violet.

Violet was standing next to a large cardboard box which had been placed on top of the folding table in the ballroom. Dressed in a pair of grey wool trousers, a white Egyptian cotton blouse, a pale blue v-neck cashmere jumper, and a pair of black Chelsea boots, Violet tilted her reading glasses back on her head of glossy blonde hair and looked for additional instructions on her smartphone.

'It can't be that difficult, Vava,' said the diminutive, flaxen haired, and now slender Poppy as she exited the temporary bedroom. Poppy, in a pair of dark khaki wool trousers, a white blouse (with a large collar), and a beige wool jumper, smiled. Poppy, after months of carrying the twins, was now enjoying being relatively slim once more. She had given birth just three weeks earlier. Yes, the birth had been two weeks early, and Poppy had come close to death, but she had survived, and the twins were healthy. God had blessed Poppy and her family.

'I'm sure Hector would be able to put it together quickly,' said Poppy happily. 'How about we go for a walk, Vava?'

Violet looked up from her smartphone. 'Are you sure you are up to it? What did the doctor say this morning?'

'He said it would be alright if I started taking walks, as long as I don't push myself too hard.'

Violet smiled. 'Alright, I'll get my coat.'

'This will be a chance to wear the cape that Gula bought me,' said Poppy.

THE CASTLE RUINS

Poppy put on the gorgeous dark purple cashmere wool cape. The dark purple cape was double breasted with six tortoise shell buttons and a fur collar. The neck of the cape could be tied with a lavender ribbon. The cape was lined with lavender silk lining. The embroidered blue label inside included a large 'KV'. It was a beautifully made garment. The attention to detail was amazing.

There was a detachable fur hood that could be buttoned onto the cape. It was made of mink. The fur hood was gorgeous and it was lined with quilted purple fabric. It could also be tied with a lavender ribbon. Poppy quickly attached the fur hood to the cape. She then put the cape on. It looked fantastic. Poppy's angelic face and blonde hair were enveloped in the fur collar and hood. Poppy smiled.

Violet buttoned up her dark blue wool coat and carefully wrapped the blue, red, and purple wool All Saints scarf around her neck and shoulders. Violet looked at her reflection in the large mirror in Poppy's temporary bedroom. Violet looked good. And she knew it.

'I haven't seen you wear your All Saints scarf since we were school girls, Vava. It looks really nice on you.'

'Thank you, Poppy. Of course, I kept the school scarf. All Saints was the happiest time of my life. I happened to find this in my closet the night I drove from Northumberland with Hughie. I took finding it as a sign. I packed it in my suitcase carried it down to the car. Well, I didn't carry my suitcase down to the car, the footman did.'

Poppy laughed. 'I love you, Vava.'

'And I love you, Poppy.'

THE DRAWING ROOM
The two Inseparables walked down the hallway, turned left, and made their
way to the drawing room. Poppy opened the door and both of them
entered.

Poppy's mother, the baroness, Holly, the nanny, and Helen were sitting in
the drawing room. Poppy's children were now in the protective arms of her
mother and sister-in-law. There cribs stood near the purple velvet sofa were
the baroness and Helen sat. Holly, her blue uniform (with a large white
collar) sat in one of the purple Art Deco chairs near the sofa.

'Poppy. Violet,' said the baroness quietly as the girls entered. 'Waverly and
Arthur have been so good today. Now they are sleeping like angels.'

The baroness held the tiny infant Waverly in her arms. Her soft, downy
blonde hair had grown thicker in the last three weeks. The baroness smiled.
'They are pure love, Poppy.'

Poppy, in her dark purple cape and mink hood, slowly and carefully walked
around the coffee table and looked down at her infant daughter. Poppy
reached out with her soft, manicured hand and gently, very gently, brushed
Waverly's blonde hair. 'Yes, they are little angels, aren't they?'

'Arthur has been a good little boy,' said Helen quietly. Helen, her long,
glossy blonde hair worn over one shoulder, smiled gently. 'He is so sweet.
He smiles a lot.'

Violet walked around behind the sofa, and hovering over Arthur said, 'Yes,
Arthur is beautiful. I sure Külli is looking forward to having the twins to
lunch at Marble Arch,' said Violet. 'I'm looking forward to having them at
the house in Northumberland.'

'This Christmas will be the happiest we have ever had,' said the baroness
quietly. 'My little Poppy and her babies are safe and healthy and here with

me. I am glad you all are her with us. Violet, thank you for staying with us. You have been a big help to the family.'

And Violet smiled.

WINTER IN THE LAKE DISTRICT

The castle ruins were only a short distance from the family pile. A thin layer of snow covered the ground. The snow had stopped earlier that morning. The entire area was covered in a beautiful white blanket of snow. The sky was mostly blue; a few white clouds drifted through the air like snow-clad mountains. The glorious and fiery Sun warmed the two friends as they walked towards the castle. The cold, crisp air was invigorating for Poppy. She was happy to be outside after a nearly three weeks of indoor confinement.

The imposing castle loomed up before them. Fifteen minutes after leaving the house, they reached the grey stone outer walls of the medieval structure.

The castle wasn't very large at all. It had probably only held a couple of hundred men when fully garrisoned. The walls, built approximately 900 years ago, were still largely intact. Of the five towers, only one remained standing. The others had collapsed long ago. The medieval stones had been carted away to be used on other structures over the centuries, including the current house which stood close by. All that remained of the internal structures were the foundations.

Poppy and Violet, the fresh snow crunching underfoot, entered the castle through the main gate. The inner courtyard looked like a large white duvet. Poppy stopped and breathed in the cold air once more.

'What a beautiful winter day,' said Poppy. 'Do you remember James and his friends from Oxford playing cricket in the castle when we were teenagers?'

'Yes! I clearly remember watching the cricket matches from the top of the tower. How wonderful it is to be young,' replied Violet happily.

Poppy smiled. 'Yes. I remember Gula wearing James' Eton cricket blazer. It barely fit her at fifteen. She must of have been two feet taller than me when we were thirteen.'

'Gula was so glossy looking with her dark brown hair and slender figure. Gula was a stunner at fifteen, and she became even more beautiful with each passing year.'

'And Gemma was the most beautiful girl at All Saints. I remember the stir she caused when she returned from the summer holiday when she was sixteen. Gemma had transformed over the summer,' said Poppy.

'I think we all had,' said Violet impishly.

'Yes, that's true. I remember how long your hair had grown out that summer. You started wearing it in two large pony tails. How stunning. I notice that Freya wears her hair like that sometimes. Was that at your suggestion?'

'No. Freya started doing it on her own. I guess that my DNA is stronger than I imagined it would be.'

'Freya is beautiful like her mother,' said Poppy and she smiled.

MARBLE ARCH

Külli looked through the catalog proofs on her laptop. One more time and then she would email them to the printers. The Spring-Summer 2020 catalog had turned out better than she had expected. The new girl on the design team was brilliant. The young graduate of Central St Martins had had a hard time finding employment. One internship after another had gone unrewarded. She had remained largely unemployed for three years since graduating. It was Octavia that had brought the young Margaret to Külli's attention.

Margaret, working freelance, had designed a new hunt coat for Octavia's hunt club. Octavia had been impressed with the cut and choice of materials. When Octavia submitted the design to Vahtra as a bespoke order, it had come to Külli's attention. Külli had telephoned her that afternoon and asked Margaret to come in for an interview. She was hired immediately.

Margaret was now on the second floor of the building overseeing the production of the collection. Yes, everything was going well.

Külli had made plans to attend The Ptolemies at Midlands-Hasegawa with Octavia later that month. After the play they would drive to the Cotswolds and spend Christmas with Octavia's family. She would stop by Poppy's house in the Lake District the day before and see the family. She was looking forward to seeing the infant twins, especially her goddaughter Waverly. Well, no, she was looking forward to seeing both of the twins equally. She loved them as much as she loved Poppy.

Gemma and Enoch had returned from the Lake District the night before. Gemma had telephoned and emailed her photos of Poppy, her children, and everyone else at the house. Violet looked really beautiful. She was so relaxed. Her demeanor was completely different than it had been when they were at All Saints.

Gemma, as beautiful as ever, and Enoch both looked happy and healthy in the photos. Külli was especially happy for Gemma. She had found true love. Külli was sure of it. She really liked Enoch Tara. He had lived just two blocks away from her in Marble Arch for years, and yet they had never met. She had never even heard of him until Gemma introduced him to her. Enoch was really cute and youthful. The slim and well-dressed Enoch was kind and gentle. Just like Gemma.

Mars also appeared in the photos. Külli had known him for almost thirty years. She had always liked Mars. He had been through a lot, but had remained good hearted and kind. Mars was extremely intelligent, if rather plain looking. Külli had decided to consult with him on some financial matters in January. She knew that Mars understood the markets better than anyone, perhaps even better than Enoch. Perhaps.

Mars was also Arthur's Godfather. Gula was convinced that between Enoch Tara and Mars Arthur Noel, Arthur Atherton was destined for a stellar career in the City.

Külli looked out the window of her office in Marble Arch. It was a beautiful winter day in London. The sky was partly cloudy and blue. The cold wintery air was kept at bay by the warm fire that glowed in her fireplace. Winter had definitely arrived in England. Külli was happy. She loved cold weather. Soon Külli would be back in the Cotswolds. There was nothing like the cold, fresh country air of England.

Gemma—The Carthage Option—The Gherkin

LONDON

Gemma, in a white blouse and a dark blue pencil skirt, was walking around her desk in the offices of Millennium Investments on the 12th floor of the Gherkin in the heart of the City in London. She had her smartphone in one hand and a document in the other. It was midday. The glorious blue skies of a cold wintery day in December could be seen outside the curved glass windows of the glassy, helix-shaped skyscraper. The panoramic views of London from the windows that surrounded Gemma and her co-workers were phenomenal. Natural light filled the offices; that alone had helped lift the spirits of the beleaguered staff hard at work within the glass walls of the circular office.

'Yes, Jemima is on the way to the airport now, Mr Lee…Her flight leaves Heathrow at 1pm…Yes, she will give the presentation to the clients when she arrives in Singapore…Alright…I'll have Allegra email you the report immediately, Mr Lee…Yes…I know…Yes, Alexa is aware of it…I will make sure she gets the report…Alright…Thank you.'

Gemma touched the screen of her phone and the call ended. Gemma exhaled. It was only 11:39am and it had already been a long day. Gemma placed her cell phone on top of her desk. Gemma, the sunlight reflecting off of her white blouse (with a large collar and open cuffs) walked over to Jemima's desk. She opened one of the drawers and searched through it. Here it is, the report. She took it out of the drawer and opened it to the index. Yes, this is the right one. She closed the desk drawer and walked towards Alexa's office.

'Allegra, could you please email Mr Lee in Singapore? He needs the information on the project.'

'Sure, Gemma. I'll do it right now.'

'Thank you.'

Gemma stopped for a moment and looked at the view of London which surrounded her. Gemma took it all in. It is important that one not let life go by without stopping to appreciate the little things. This view, for instance. How many people were fortunate enough to have a view like this? How many people, even in London, would have the opportunity to see the city from here? Very few. The panoramic views of London from the 12th floor in the daytime were beautiful, equally so at night. Gemma scanned the skyline for another minute. Every time she did so, she noticed some new detail of the city.

Gemma turned and continued on to Alexa's office. She gently knocked on the door.

'Come in,' said Alexa.

Gemma entered. Alexa, in a white blouse and looking well rested, sat at her desk behind piles of reports, large and small envelopes, documents, three different smartphones, and a tablet computer. Alexa's blonde hair was tied back with a white silk ribbon. She was noticeably thinner. Her complexion was glowing. Alexa smiled.

'Good afternoon, Gemma.'

Gemma smiled. 'You look great, Alexa. A good night's rest, or two, has done wonders for you.'

Alexa smiled and said, 'Thank you, Gemmy. You were right. I needed to get some sleep. A few healthy meals made by my daughter Sarah, and I feel great.'

'It's nice to see you smile again, Alexa. Oh, here is the report. Mr Lee asked me a moment ago to make sure you had a copy of it.'

'Once Jemima has given her presentation, the clients should calm down somewhat. She's extremely intelligent and understands the situation as well as anyone here,' said Alexa.

'Yes. Jemima was a good envoy to send to Asia. She will relax in Singapore for two days after the presentation and then fly to Tokyo.'

'Yes, that's good. Jemima needs a break. We all do. How are you feeling, Gemma?'

'I'm good. I visited Poppy in the Lake District last weekend. The twins are healthy and happy.'

'I'm happy to hear that, Gemmy. Poppy emailed some photos of herself and the twins. Poppy looks great. Mars looks great too. He looks happy. How is Mars?'

'He's good. He was on holiday last week in the Lake District. He has a house in Cumbria. He is sharing godparenting responsibilities with me and Enoch. Enoch loves children. The twins both seemed quite taken with him.'

Alexa arched an eyebrow. Yes, that's right. Enoch Tara was there with The Honourable Gemma Ophelia Ripley. And he was in the same room with Lord Mars Arthur Noel, the 13th Baron. They were the godparents of Arthur Henry Atherton. Yes, of course Enoch and Mars talked about what was going on in the City. Of course, they did. Was Gemma privy too it? No. No way. Enoch would keep her on the other side of the veil as long as she worked for Millennium Investments. Still, that bit of information was of interest. Alexa was unsure if Gemma realized the significance of it. Probably not. Gemma had been friends with Mars since she was thirteen. Mars was practically part of Poppy's family. Or maybe Gemma did realize the importance of them meeting unexpectantly last weekend?

'How is Poppy?' asked Alexa.

'Much better. She has lost most of her baby weight and is eating healthy and getting plenty of sleep. Violet is staying with her.'

'Violet and Poppy sharing a room? Just like All Saints,' said Alexa laughingly.

'Yes, I asked them if they had had any popcorn and movie nights. Poppy said that after she returned to London, she would invite people over to her house for popcorn and movie nights. Poppy plans to return to work in a few months,' said Gemma.

'Will she return to London with the twins?'

'Yes. Brian is overseeing the finishing touches on the nursery at Poppy's house in Covent Garden this week. Brian visits Poppy at least once a week. He takes the train in the morning and returns the next day.'

How are Poppy's parents?'

'Much better. They are happy to have Poppy and the twins at home with them. The family is happy. Helen is also very helpful. And Henry and Lucy are so sweet; they are excited about having cousins, and they help their mother and their Aunt Poppy whenever they can.'

When Gemma talked about children, her face always lit up. Gemma hadn't been able to have children; something she had always wanted. Alexa remembered Gemma talking about her future children the first time they had met at All Saints when they were both only thirteen. It wasn't fair. It wasn't.

'And I plan to spend Christmas with the family this year. At least part of the holiday. I'm going to spend the holidays at my country house. Well, a few days, at least. Enoch wants to spend Christmas day with his mother in Surrey. I plan to spend it with them. Enoch's mother is very kind. And she is a good cook.'

Alexa smiled. 'I'm happy everything is going so well, Gemma.'

'What are you doing for Christmas this year?' asked Gemma.

'Alastair is flying home to England for the holidays. The girls will be happy to see him. We are going to spend it at the cottage in the Cotswolds. It will be nice to just relax for a few days.'

'Yes. It will. Have you decided who will run the office while we are out?' asked Gemma.

'Yes, the office in Singapore will handle everything for a few days. Tarquin and Allegra will return on December 28th along with Isolde and Helen. We will both return on January 3rd. We might have to work that Saturday.'

'Noted,' said Gemma happily.

3 MERCIA

Gemma—The Carthage Option— Spem in alium

MERICA
Ping.

Wren stirred in bed. The camp bed was warm and surprisingly comfortable. The thin mattresses were new, so were the white sheets and pillows. Wren's mother had purchased them on sale. The wool blankets had been taken from the family linen closet. They were used constantly in the winter months.

The fire in the fireplace was now a glowing pile of embers and ash, but it still generated a little heat. The girls had positioned their beds around the fireplace to stay warm. (And to fight off any spectres.) Natural light filled the room, along with the electrical lights from the lamps that the girls had left on.

Wren reached under the covers and searched for her smartphone. There it is. She looked at it. It was 8:01am. She had a message. She tapped on the screen.

'Are you coming down for breakfast? We have made you something

special. – Mummy

Wren was half asleep, but even in that state, she felt a burst of happiness and love surge through her. Her parents were doing everything they could to make Wren's weekend visit with her friends special. Because Wren's parents loved her as much as she loved them.

Wren rolled onto her side and looked over at the other girls. All of them were still asleep.

Ping.

'We have hot water.'

Wren smiled. She got up and looked outside. It was overcast. It would start snowing soon. She got out of bed and put on her slippers. She stretched. She walked over to the glossy white door to the bathroom, opened it, entered, and closed the door behind her.

Wren took a quick shower. She didn't want to use all of the hot water. Standing in the white enameled, cast-iron Victorian bathtub, Wren thought about what they would do first after breakfast while shampooing her honey blonde hair.

When Wren stepped out of the bathroom with her wet hair wrapped in a white towel and wearing a white cotton bathrobe, the other girls were sitting on the edge of their beds.

'I saved all of you some hot water,' said Wren happily. She felt great.

'Who is next?' asked Wren.

The girls looked at each other. No one wanted to be the one to ask. Wren smiled and decided for them. 'Jinx, you're next. There is a stack of fresh towels on the marble sink top.'

Jinx, smiled, nodded, stood up, and entered the bathroom.

THE KITCHEN

Wren's parents had prepared a fantastic breakfast for the girls. For the more health conscious, there were slices of fresh fruit on a sterling silver tray and a glass bottle of cold milk from the local dairy. For the not so health conscious, there was an English fry up of scrambled eggs, toast, bacon, sausage, baked beans, grilled tomatoes, and fried Portobello mushrooms. No one was feeling particularly health conscious that morning. Freya enjoyed breakfast more than any other meal. Seated at the wooden table in the kitchen in the manor house surrounded by walls of ancient grey stone and with natural daylight flooding into the room from the paned glass windows (filled with blown glass), Freya felt calm, an English sense of calm.

The girls were all wearing wool trousers, cotton blouses, and wool jumpers. Wallis, her blonde hair piled on her head and held there with silver hairpins, obviously liked meat; her plate was filled with bacon and sausage. She also enjoyed toast and baked beans. Freya noticed Jinx eating scrambled eggs and a single piece of bacon. Perhaps the slender Jinx was trying to lose weight? Jinx was seated near Wren's mother and chatted happily with her in unrestrained Rhodesian English. Jinx, her glossy black chin length bob framing her face like a World War One German Stahlhelm, smiled often. Wren took turns talking with her father, the 23rd Baron, Wallis, and Freya.

Wren's father reminded Freya of her wayward cousin Septimus in some respects. He was blonde, slender, posh, and handsome. The baron was also very polite and well spoken. He talked about his love of hunting wild boar, which Wallis loved to do too. Freya couldn't get over how youthful Wren's parents were. Amazing. Then again, Freya's mother Violet was easily as youthful as Wren's mother. Freya said very little at breakfast. She was content to enjoy the breakfast fare and try to decide which of Wren's parents Wren resembled the most.

THE VILLAGE

A few inches of snow had fallen overnight. The Bristol Mark II was covered in a thin layer of snow. The village, just beyond the manor, was blanketed in snow, a white ocean. It was really quite beautiful. (Yes, that's the best way to describe it.) The branches of the trees sagged under the weight of the snow. The roof tops of the village could be seen just a hundred yards beyond the trees. The girls decided to walk into the village.

Freya put on her blue quilted jacket and her red, blue, and purple All Saints school scarf. Jinx put on her dark grey wool jacket, a dark blue knitted cap and her dark blue scarf (with a thick white stripe down the center) from The Borders school. Wallis wore a pair of dark blue wool trousers, a thick, oversized, heather grey wool jumper (over a white cotton blouse and a thin, pale blue, wool, v-neck sweater), and beige wool scarf that she was able to wrap around her head and shoulder twice, her blonde hair still piled on her head. Wren, the future 24th Baroness, wore dark khaki wool trousers, brown Chelsea boots, a dark blue wool coat (with silver buttons), and a thick beige wool scarf. Wren was also wearing a Harris Tweed (dark blue, light blue, and light grey tartan) Cossack style hat (with a six-panel top) with deep fur cuff. Wren always dressed well when she entered the village—even if she were wearing a pair of faded blue jeans. She was, after all, the future baroness. All of the girls wore wool gloves.

The single lane road to the village was paved with cobblestones. The road the teenage undergraduates walked had existed in the same place (more or less) since the baron's ancestors had arrived in the area over 900 years ago. The village had always been small. The castle on the hill had protected it in times of danger. It had been for that very reason that the Roundheads had destroyed it. Most of the adult male population had been killed in the fighting by the time the New Model Army arrived. The last men in the village were killed trying to protect the manor house and castle. The baron was faraway the day the Parliamentarians arrived—lying badly wounded in a farm house. The surviving villagers—women and children—watched helplessly as the soldiers destroyed the ancient structures. The villagers, all loyal, searched through the wrecked manor house and retrieved what they could. They hid what they could find in a cave nearby.

A few months after the King had been beheaded, the Royalist prisoners were released and made their way back to the village. The villagers returned to their farms and waited for the rightful rulers to return to England. They would wait for a decade. And then, one day, news from London. The King had returned. Certainly, the baron would return too. Wouldn't he?

Two months after the King of England had ascended the throne, the elderly baron appeared at the entrance of the village. The frail old man, dressed in threadbare clothes, had accepted an offer in London to accompany a wool merchant in his wagon. The old man, with white hair and a pronounced limp, walked slowly through the village on that cold morning on a day in October.

The first person to recognize him was the village blacksmith. Yes, it was the baron. He had returned. But he was all alone. His son had been killed in battle and his wife, the baroness, had died in Holland; the harshness of their poverty having been too much for her. The baron's only surviving child, a daughter, had disappeared. The baron had assumed she was dead, until three days later when she too appeared at the edge of the village.

A local farmer invited the baron and his youngest daughter (there had been three, but only one survived the civil war) to occupy his house until the manor could be repaired. The farmer moved in with his son-in-law. The baron had initially refused, but the farmer and the son-in-law had insisted he stay in the house.

The elderly baron, his property restored to him by the crown, was forced to sell most of the remaining farm land to rebuild the manor house. After a year, the baron was able to move back into the partially rebuilt manor. He died a few months later. It was his iron-willed daughter, the new baroness, that turned the former medieval manor into a Jacobean country house. It was the baroness's business acumen that allowed the family to install the marble staircase and fireplace. She married the youngest son of a wealthy landowner who also manufactured silk buttons and produced wool cloth. They had a daughter who would go on to become the next baroness. The baroness's bond with the villagers was as strong as iron. That bond had remained till this day. Outsiders, especially Londoners, could not grasp that such loyalty still existed in the modern world.

Wren and her family were attached to the land. Though they now owned very little of it, Wren still considered the surrounding lands to be an extension of herself.

The four girls walked along the edge of the road, the snow crunching under their feet. The sky was overcast; a swirl of white and grey eddied above them. The tall ancient trees, their branches shrouded in snow, swayed in the cold winds. Freya pulled her scarf up over half her face. Only her blue eyes appeared under her glossy blonde bangs.

The girls walked, following the bending road until, after a few minutes, the village came into view. The first house was made of white washed stone and had a thatched roof. Smoke rose from its chimney. Three houses stood on the other side of the cobblestone street, all three had slate roofs. Several large trees grew in the village; in the summer the cobblestone streets of the village were all heavily shaded. Parked in front of one of the houses was a dark blue 1995 Land Rover Defender.

The girls continued to walk down the deserted road. Another minute and the village fountain appeared in the main square. The stone fountain was filled with snow. Around the square were the local pub, (The Georgian pub had been constructed on the foundations of a Tudor pub, which had been constructed on the foundations of—well, you get the idea), a book store (with a stone-tile roof), a fabric shop, and a stone building with a slate roof, a former button factory, which now housed the village cricket club. Smoke rose from the chimney of the pub. A woman, in a pale blue wool jumper, could be seen moving about inside the fabric shop.

The girls walked past the stone fountain and a family-owned butcher shop came into view. Inside the white walled store, two people, one a middle-aged man, the other a young woman, in white dress shirts and long blue aprons (with vertical white stripes) and straw boater hats, were behind the counter serving several customers in parkas and quilted jackets.

The girls continued to walk. To their right was a red 1967 BMC Mini Copper S parked in front of a stone house with a slate roof. Parked behind it was a silver 1987 Nissan Micra.

They walked farther down the paved cobblestone street until the girls reached one edge of the village; here was the local dairy. The long white washed stone building with a slate roof that had a shop at one end with large windows that could be entered through a bright blue wooden door. The opposite end of the building had two sets of large, wooden double doors that once housed the dairy's delivery carts. The dairy had been here since 1893. The same family still owned and operated it. The long building housed modern pasteurization machinery and produced bottled milk. Fresh milk was delivered daily via the dairy's white delivery van.

Most of the houses in the village were over a century old, some were centuries old. The houses had been passed down through generations. Virtually every resident of the village owned farmland which they either farmed themselves or leased to others. Just beyond the ancient trees, thousands of sheep and herds of cattle wondered the pastures which surrounded the village.

THE ANGLICAN CHURCH

The village's medieval Anglican grey stone church was not only a spiritual sanctuary, but the social center of the village. The local vicar, an elderly priest who had been born in the village, attended seminary in Durham, worked as a missionary in India, and as priest in churches all over England, had returned in his old age, was kind and welcoming. The vicar and his wife would host luncheons and teas at the Edwardian vicarage which was on the other side of the cemetery.

The Perpendicular Late Gothic church had been constructed entirely out of stone. The church's ribbed vault ceiling consisted of four-centred arches. Inside the large stone church (unusually large considering the size of the village) was an altar of stone, wooden box pews (that could seat three hundred parishioners), and a dozen stone tomb effigies of Wren's noble ancestors. Some of the armour effigies were of alabaster, others of grey stone; the stonemasons had taken great care to show the minute details of the armour and swords that the barons had worn and carried. The stone tomb effigies were identifiable not only by the chain mail and surcoats, shields and swords, but by the names and the family coat of arms that had been carved into the large sarcophagi in Latin. Over a dozen ledger stones, inscribed stone slabs, had been laid into the floor along the walls of the church. The slab stones had been decorated with relief-sculpted or incised coats of arms. The interior of the church was entirely medieval. It had been built by Wren's distant ancestor, the 1st Baron, at enormous expense. The church was a symbol of his devotion (and immense wealth). When there was no more room in the church to intern members of the baronial family, ornately carved tombstones marked where the family members had been buried in the cemetery that surrounded the church.

The cemetery covered almost three acres and was heavily shaded by ancient trees in the summer. During the summer, the cemetery appeared to be a small forest; the Anglican church was barely visible behind the trees. Several large stone vaults could be seen near the side gate of the cemetery. Some belonged to Wren's family, others belonged to wealthy merchants and farmers that had been born, lived out their lives, and died in the village environs. Most of the village dead had been buried in common graves. The cemetery was now full. No plots had been available since 1923. Unless, of course, you were a member of the baronial family. There was still an unused section along the south wall. One day, thought Wren, she would rest there with her ancestors. The villagers still carefully tended to the graves of their long dead ancestors. Fresh flowers were often left on the tombstones of family that had died over five hundred years ago.

Church attendance remained strong. Wren and her parents always attended when at home.

The churchyard was surrounded by houses on all sides. A few of the houses were two-storeys high and belonged to the descendants of wealthy merchant families.

The outer edges of the village gave way to green pastures that were dotted with stone wells, large trees, cottages, the occasional barely store, and a medieval tithe barn. It was in this very barn that the baron had marshalled the villagers in support of King Charles I. It was here that the baron, his son, and other cavaliers, had trained the locals and turned them into soldiers. Most would perish in the English Civil War, often dying at the baron's side. The tithe barn was now owned by a wealthy local farmer who had paid to restore it. It was used for village events.

Freya was impressed. The medieval village was picture postcard beautiful. Wallis loved it. She expected to see figures from the Canterbury Tales appear at any moment. Jinx felt like she had travelled back in time. With the exception of cars parked here and there, the village looked like it had been virtually untouched in 900 years. And all of it was freezing under a white blanket of snow.

The girls stood on the edge of the village; before them stood a forest of tall ancient trees. The forest began at the base of a hill. The entire hill was heavily forested and now choked with snow. The sky had grown darker and the temperature had started to drop.

'Believe it or not, behind those trees and at the top of the hill, is my ancestral castle. Would you like to see it?' said Wren, her breath materializing in the icy cold weather. Wren's shiny and glossy honey blonde hair, which poked out from under the fur Cossack cap, shimmered in the grey, white, and overcast conditions.

'I'm game,' said Wallis, through chattering teeth.

'Are you sure that you will be warm enough, Wallis?' asked Wren.

'I'm under three layers. I'll be warm enough,' said Wallis, and she smiled.

'Alright. There is a path up to the castle, but I haven't been up it since last summer. It will be hard to see the path under all of this snow. Please follow me and be careful,' said Wren.

Wren walked into the forest; the girls all followed. They made their way through the trees as they walked around the base of the hill. They reached a small clearing. Wren walked across it and started to climb up the snow covered hill. The wind picked up as the four teenage undergraduates ascended. The snow crunched under foot as they climbed.

Occasionally one of them would slip on the snow and ice. Thin fallen branches snapped under foot; the sounds reminded Freya of the night that she and Louise had escaped from All Saints and walked slowly and carefully through the forest with two of Grey's men looking for them on that winter night almost a year ago. The events of that night now seemed surreal to her. It was almost as if it had happened to someone else. The escape had been a close one. One false move and they would have been taken. A brief lapse in faith, and they both would have surrendered and been taken. Neither would have survived. Freya and Louise both realized that as soon as the two young men appeared outside their dormitory. Freya and Louise had not really spoken of it since that night. Gemma and Freya had only spoken of those events a few times, and only fleetingly. Freya shuddered involuntarily. It was not the cold; it was Freya reliving that night as she walked up the hill on an overcast day in December in Mercia.

THE CASTLE

The four girls reached the summit of the hill after a fifteen-minute ascent through the snowy woods. Before them stood the ruins of Wren's ancestral castle. It had once had eight towers. Only three of the towers still stood; the other five were piles of stone blocks. The Grade I listed stone structure had been largely demolished. A rough outline of the medieval walls existed as a line of foundation and tumbled stones. Parts of the walls did partially exist in sections. The interior castle structures still existed, though some were badly damaged. The snow-clad castle ruins looked like a pile of wooden blocks thrown about on the floor of nursery by an angry toddler. Only the blocks were of grey stone and not so easily put away. It was obvious to Freya that this had once been a huge and formidable castle.

'Yes,' said Wren. 'It used to tower over the village.'

'Our castle is in a similar state,' said Wallis. 'What they did to us. What they did to the King. It's horrible.'

Jinx adjusted her (mostly) dark blue wool scarf. She examined the ruins carefully. Jinx tried to visualize what the castle must once have looked like. Now none of it existed above the tree line. It was invisible from the village. The ruins were awe inspiring.

Freya was surprised at the size the castle. It was easily three times the size of Poppy's castle in the Lake District. Poppy's castle, while a partial ruin, was in much better condition. The castle had only been spared by the Roundheads because it had already fallen into disrepair by the time of the English Civil War. Poppy's family had also supported the king. Poppy's family had paid a high price too.

'Come on, let's go inside,' said Wren. Wren's breath could be easily seen in the wintery air.

Wren, the future 24th Baroness and owner of the castle, led the way through the ruined gate house. The four girls made their way through the ruins leaving a trail of footprints in the snow behind them. They reached a stone building in the center of the castle ruins and stopped. The entrance to the building was a pair of large wooden double doors. The Jacobean doors were heavily weathered. The stone building appeared to be undamaged.

HOPE IN ANY OTHER HAVE I NONE
Wren turned to face the girls and said, 'Yes, the doors are Jacobean, not Medieval. The family had the originals installed in 1628. They have been periodically replaced throughout the centuries. The doors you see now were installed in 1913. This building was left untouched by the Roundheads. When we go inside, you will see why.'

Wren pushed on the doors and they opened. Natural light partially (mostly) illuminated the interior. Wren turned on the lamp in her smartphone and stepped inside. The other girls turned on their smartphones lamps and followed her.

Beams of light from the four smartphones illuminated parts of the room that the natural light from the entrance did not. Wren pointed her smartphone lamp towards the ceiling. The ceiling was smooth stone that had been covered in a fresh coat of white paint. There were Jacobean sash windows on either side of the chapel, but they were shuttered. The austere altar was of grey stone. The wall behind the altar was made up of weathered hand carved Jacobean oak panels. A carved wooden Jacobean pulpit, accompanied by an ornamental tester, stood to the right of the stone altar. On either side of the room were heavily weathered looking wooden box pews. The freshly painted white walls were smooth stone. The chapel could hold around fifty people.

'The Roundheads did not damage the Anglican chapel. My family had this part of the castle converted into an Anglican chapel during the reign of Charles I. We held services here until 1914. The war interrupted everything. For some reason, the family stopped using it. I really don't know why. The electric lights used to work. But that was a long time ago. Some of the panes of glass in the windows were handblown over a hundred years ago. The others were replacements from the 1960s. One day I will repair the lights and have services held here. I will also have the doors and wooden pews restored. Over there is the baptismal font.'

The chapel was remarkably clean.

'It was my job to come in here and sweep the chapel out once a week. My parents do it now. We do what we can to maintain it. They painted the walls a few weeks ago. They did it themselves. Mummy is really good at painting interiors. In the summer, we like to come up here and have picnic in the chapel. We don't want to let it rot apart. It is important to the family.'

The girls walked around the stone room. It was a Jacobean room in a medieval structure. A cold wind whipped through the chapel from outside. Wallis tried to warm herself by crossing her arms and rubbing her shoulders.

'The Roundheads never found the tunnel,' said Wren nonchalantly.

'What? There was a tunnel?' asked Freya.

'Yes,' said Wren.

At that moment Wren was standing in the natural light which came in through the double doors. Yes, this was the future 24th Baroness in her element. The slender Wren's long, honey blonde hair and bangs, which partially covered her blue eyes, made her look like a French film actress in the 1950s. Only Wren was English and Rhodesian. And it was 2019.

'The tunnel was built the same time as the castle in the 1300s. Would you like to see it?' asked Wren.

'Yes, *rather*!' said Jinx excitedly in her Rhodesian Sloane intonation.

'Alight. But, girls; you have to keep it a secret.'

'*Okay, yah*!' said Jinx happily.

Wren walked past the baptismal font of carved stone and behind the altar. She stopped and pushed on one of the wooden panels; the wall moved inwards. Wren then carefully and gently slid the panel open to reveal a small stone room.

Wren pointed the smartphone lamp into the small stone chamber. She turned and smiled. 'Alright. Follow me.'

Wren lifted a weathered wooden hatch with an iron ring in it. A set of carved circular stone stairs wide enough for one person at a time to descend them was below. A cold rush of air came up from the hole in the floor.

'I'll go first. Be careful, the floor can be slippery.'

Wren made her ways down the steps until her head disappeared into the darkness. Jinx looked down into the hole; the lamp of her smartphone illuminated the smooth grey stone walls and steps. It was impossible to look down the spiraling and enclosed staircase.

'I'll go,' said Jinx.

Freya followed. Wallis made her way down the steps last. It was cold and dark. The only light was the narrow beams of light from their smartphones. It only took about a minute to reach the bottom of the stairs. The tunnel was constructed of ashlar stone. The tunnel was an engineering marvel. The floor was paved smooth stone. The tunnel was dark and about ten feet wide and eight feet high. It was difficult to determine how long it was, but there was a bit of natural daylight coming from the end of the tunnel.

'This was used to secretly supply the fortress during sieges. Or to escape,' said Wren.

'Is it safe to be down here?' asked Jinx.

'Yes. These walls have been here since the 1300s.'

'How long is the tunnel?' asked Freya while shining her smartphone lamp down the tunnel.

'Two hundred and three yards,' replied Wren.

'This place is amazing, Wren,' said Wallis through chattering teeth.

'Yes, we think so too,' said Wren happily, and she smiled.

Jinx touched the cold stone wall. She wondered about the lives of the people who had been through this tunnel. Had any of them ever really known happiness?

'Shall we?' asked Wren.

Wren led the way down the smooth stone tunnel. The stone echoed under their feet as they walked. The small beams of their smartphone lamps flashed around them like bolts of lightning. An icy wind occasionally gusted down the long, dark stone tunnel as they moved closer to the end of it. Further down the tunnel, the natural light grew brighter and more discernable. Yes, the exit was a large single heavy ironbound oak door. It was heavily weathered and partially rotted away; natural light entered the tunnel through the holes in the door.

'The door hasn't been replaced since the 1940s. We have always built exact copies of it. Wren slide the iron bolt back with some difficulty and opened the door inward. The exterior of the door was weathered and rotted. Natural light flooded into the tunnel exit. The tunnel opened onto a heavily wooded part of the hill slope that was shrouded in trees and covered in snow and dead branches.

'There were steps carved into the earth a few decades ago. My father used to climb up and down them when he very young. They were not maintained and so the rain turned them to mud and washed them away. The door was smeared with mud during the siege. This area is not easily accessible. Our enemies never discovered the exit or the tunnels. Not even the Roundheads.'

Jinx, Wallis, Wren, and Freya stood on the stone ledge inside the tunnel and looked down the steeply sloping hillside. No, it would not be easy to go down it.

'I'm freezing. I think it's time to go back to the house,' said Wren.

Jinx looked at her inexpensive quartz watch: 2:34pm. 'We missed lunch. I didn't realize how long we have been out here.'

'Yes, time flies in a castle,' said Wren in her posh intonation.

Gemma—The Carthage Option—The Snowy Hill

THE CASTLE RUINS
The hillside was far too steep for the girls to exit the castle ruins through the secret tunnel. Wren closed the large door (which opened inward) and locked it with the large iron sliding bolt lock. Once again, the girls were standing in a long dark tunnel with only the narrow beams of light from their smartphones to light the way.

'There is another way down the hill. It used to be a road, but four hundred years of neglect and rain have left it a long ditch,' said Wren, her strikingly beautiful face illuminated in the pale lamplight of the smartphones. Wren turned and began to walk down the long, narrow, stone tunnel. It was freezing cold; not even the warm clothing, heavy scarves, and gloves could keep the cold at bay any longer.

The girls climbed the spiral stone staircase and emerged back into the chapel. The large, wooden double doors had been left wide open and a few flakes of snow could be seen swirling around in the wind outside. It was starting to snow. Wren secured the secret door. The girls left the chapel and Wren carefully closed the weathered Jacobean double doors behind them.

The four girls trudged through the falling snow, careful to step over or walk around the pieces of stone which were scattered throughout the grounds of the castle ruins.

'No, not that way, Freya. Over here. This way,' said Wren as she motioned for the other girls to follow her. Wren climbed up and then stood on top of the foundation of one of the toppled walls. The girls climbed up and joined her. This section of the former wall faced away from the village. Beyond, the girls saw a vast expanse of white landscape. The hill was heavily forested; however, most of the trees swayed leaflessly in the cold wind. The view was nothing less than spectacular. The snow-covered fields and hills stretched for as far as the eye could see.

'Be careful going down the hill. The snow will hide most of the ruts and holes. Try to follow in my footsteps,' said Wren.

The former road was still there, even four centuries after the castle had been left a complete ruin by the New Model Army. Ancient trees lined either side of the dirt road. It was wide enough to have a dozen men walk abreast up it. Dead leaves and snow crunched underfoot and small dead branches snapped as the girls made their way down the hill. The girls walked for a few minutes, and then, half way down, the skies seemed to open and dump snow on the four undergraduates. A minute later and the girls could no longer make out the terrain ahead. The temperature was dropping rapidly.

'Don't worry. There is shelter at the bottom of the hill,' said Wren.

Freya, Jinx, Wren, and Wallis were freezing. Jinx looked ahead and could make out some dark shapes at the base of the hill. Some small buildings were down there. Wren slipped a few times as she made her way down the hillside; all the girls slipped and slid a little as they walked. The buildings below appeared as long dark shapes in the heavy snow, nothing more.

THE NISSEN HUTS

The pre-fabricated, curved corrugated steel huts were sixteen feet in diameter and thirty-six feet long. There were two of them to the right of the girls and one to the left. Tall trees grew between and behind them. Wren walked toward the hut closest to the girls on the right. The girls, frozen to the bone, stumbled after her. Wren reached the door, took out some keys, unlocked the door, and opened it. Wren walked inside and turned on the lights. The girls filed in after her.

The interior of the Nissen hut consisted of long wooden plank flooring and corrugated metal walls that had been painted white. The ends of the hut were covered in horizontal wooden boards that had also been painted white. There were two wooden doors at the end of the hut opposite the entrance. There were at least a dozen folding metal chairs stacked up against the wall at the end of the long room. Three worn wooden tables were placed at different points in the hut. There was also a wooden desk, a grey metal filing cabinet, an old white refrigerator, and a large wooden wardrobe.

'The huts were put all put up in one day in October, 1939, by the army. This was a training base. The woods behind the castle were where the soldiers would learn how to fight in dense forests. There used to be a dozen of these huts. After the war, the Ministry of Defense leased this plot of land around the castle from us to continue training. The Territorial Army took it over in the 1950s and trained here until 1992. The MoD lease provided the family with a steady income for decades. The village also had over a hundred hungry soldiers at their doorsteps. The pub was always crowded and so were the four restaurants and the other village shops. Now the there are only two restaurants and the pub is only crowded on the weekends,' said Wren and she walked over to the wooden desk.

The girls were still freezing. But, at least, they were out of the falling snow. Wren pulled a room heater out the desk well. She picked it up and then placed it in front of the desk. She picked up the long black electrical cord and plugged it into the wall socket. Within seconds, the heater began to glow; the girls all gathered around the orange light. The heater worked well.

'The MoD was going to take down all of the huts, but my grandfather asked the ministry to leave a few of them behind. The army upgraded the huts over the years. My family uses them for the local hunt club. The hut across from us was used for briefings and has a movie screen. The army left the obsolete projector behind too. Only this hut has electricity right now. There are lavatories beyond those doors.'

THE MANOR HOUSE
'Yes, Wren. I was wondering where you were. You've been gone for over four hours…Yes, I'm glad you remembered to bring the key to hut…Alright…I'll drive out and get you…Yes…Don't worry. I'm sure the hatchback will make it…Oh, wait…Your father says he will drive out in the Riley and pick you up…Yes. It's running. Don't worry…It won't breakdown. Well, I hope not,' said the baroness laughingly.

Wren's mother hung up the phone. The baron had already put on his dark blue parka and was headed out to the stone coach house to start the black 1956 Riley Pathfinder.

THE HUT
'The hut is in really good condition,' said Freya as she adjusted herself in the folding metal chair. The girls now sat on folding metal chairs in a semi-circle around the room heater. The girls had all taken off the wool gloves and put them on the wooden desk to dry.

'The MoD took good care of them. The huts were all rewired in 1990. They soldiers use to carry full packs up and down the hill to the castle to build up their strength and endurance. The training courses usually lasted a couple of weeks. The Territorials used to train on the weekends. There was always something going on over here. There used to be a dozen huts and military vehicles parked everywhere. This is was all before I was born,' said Wren.

'What do you use the other huts for?' asked Wallis in her posh intonation. Wallis, by now, had taken off her beige wool scarf and was letting it dry on the desk near the room heater.

'Storage. Sometimes. Mostly they have sat empty for almost thirty years. We paint them once every two or three years. And we make sure there are no leaks. They are good condition. The last time I looked, one was filled with cans of paint, brushes, and bags of plaster. Things we use to repair the roof and replaster and paint the walls. The other hut had garden tools and old car parts in it. We have a couple of old cars back at the house. We sold a Thornycroft a few months ago. It had sat in the cart shed since the late 50s. Or maybe the late 60s. I can't remember for sure,' said Wren.

'What is a Thornycroft?' asked Jinx, her glossy, black, chin length bob framing her face.

'It's a truck. Thornycroft went bankrupt decades ago. My family bought it for some reason. It was a giant thing. It was built just after the Queen's ascension. I remember there was a huge letter 'T' on the front of the truck. I *rather* liked its appearance,' said the posh Wren, the Sloane Ranger, in her Sloaney intonation.

Jinx took out her smartphone. She was going to look for photos of one online. No signal.

'No. There is no signal on this side of the castle,' said Wren. 'I have photos of it back at the house. I will show them to you tonight.'

'My father restores vehicles. We have a Range Rover from the 1970s. It looks brand new now. It gets terrible mileage. We only drive it around the village,' said Jinx. 'We have a VW hatchback too.'

'Yes, we have 1995 VW Golf. Mummy bought it used while at Oxford. She bought it from another undergraduate. We've never had any problems with it,' replied Wren.

'I love cars, especially old ones,' said Wallis. 'Mummy drives a new hatchback, but I love the Bristol motorcar. If I buy another car, it will be a Bristol. Or maybe a Thornycroft.'

'Can you drive a manual transmission?' asked Wren.

'No. But I could learn,' replied Wallis.

'I think the Thornycroft had eight gears; or was it twelve? Something like that,' said Wren.

Outside the hut, the snow fell steadily, but the snow fall was lighter than it had been earlier.

'Why don't you open the castle for tours?' asked Freya.

'Tours? Of what? The castle is a pile of rubble. What interest would the average person have in seeing it?'

'Parts of the castle are still standing. A few towers and sections of the wall still stand. The gatehouse. And most of the internal structures are still there. And the chapel is fantastic. And the secret tunnel. Wren the castle is *absolutely marvellous*,' said Freya.

'You think so?' asked a clearly perplexed Wren.

'Yes, I do,' replied Freya, who was in the process of rewrapping her blue, red, and purple All Saints scarf around her shoulders.

'Yes. So do I,' said Wallis. 'Offer tours for £9.00 a head. The castle is worth at least that much,' said flaxen haired Wallis. 'Mummy charges that much to visit our small Georgian country house. And it is really just a house. Surely you could get that much for a castle with a secret tunnel and a Jacobean chapel.'

'Yes, *rather*,' said Jinx in her Rhodesian Sloane intonation. 'My family would love to visit and see the castle, the chapel, and walk through the secret tunnel. Your family could also sell souvenirs to tourists. And publish a book on the history of the castle,' said Jinx happily.

'I'll introduce you to my one of my Godmother's closest friends. Her family offers tours of their castle and they published a book on the castle and it sells fairly well. Wren your family has an interesting history,' said Freya.

Wren listened in astonishment. It had never occurred to her or (apparently) anyone in the family that anyone would be that interested in the forgotten castle ruins at the top of a hidden hill in Mercia. At least not enough people to make it worthwhile.

'We would need to provide facilities. We can't afford to build them. The National Trust asked the family to offer tours. They said they would help us. But we have always been afraid they would somehow end up taking the castle away from us,' said Wren.

'What facilities? They huts have all you need. A public restroom and a hut for souvenirs and ticket sales. You could also sell tickets online,' said Freya.

Wren arched an eyebrow. 'You really think that many people would be interested?'

'Yes!' said the other girls excitedly in near unison.

A light bulb seemed to go on over Wren's head of long, glossy honey blonde hair. Yes, it just might work.

Suddenly headlights flashed outside and a car could be heard. It was Wren's father, the baron. He had arrived to pick the girls up and drive them back to the house. The girls had missed lunch—Wren's parents had assumed they had eaten lunch at the pub. They hadn't.

The door creaked open and the baron entered. Dressed in faded blue jeans, a dark blue parka, and brown leather Oxfords, Wren's father looked more like a posh undergraduate on holiday than a middle-aged parent. He smiled.

'Are you ready go back to the house?'

'Yes. We've had *quite* the adventure this afternoon,' said Wren and she smiled.

Gemma—The Carthage Option—The Godparents

MARBLE ARCH

Enoch stood in the mirror as he tied his dark blue, red, and light grey tartan neck tie. Yes, it went well with his white dress shirt.

Gemma was planning to visit the Lake District again. She had been given Friday off. She would be staying with Poppy at her country house and spend time with the family. She had already reserved a private cabin on the train. Enoch wanted to go with her, but given the situation in the City, it was not possible.

The charts and information that Mars had gathered and taped to the walls of his cottage in Cumbria was enlightening and frightening all at the same time. Mars was brilliant, as financially savvy as he had ever been. Enoch would like to have hired him, but Mars had been banned from life from the stock market. Enoch, however, would pay him for his advice and information, somehow. A person deserves to be paid in full for his work.

Mars was on to something. He had noticed things that even Enoch had not. Mars made it all so easy to understand. Yes, a malevolent force was on the move. And yes, it was definitely someone or some group of people in London behind it all. Their motivations had remained a mystery.

Enoch was relieved that Poppy was making a quick recovery. Gemma had purchased some baby clothes for the twins at a boutique in London. Enoch had purchased two sterling silver baby combs (with white ribbons) from Asprey for the them. Gemma would give them to the family for him.

Gemma was overjoyed at the prospect of being a godmother to little Arthur. Gemma still had her goddaughter Freya, she always would, but Gemma loved children more than anyone. The infant Arthur was a pure little angel that needed all the protection and love he could get. Enoch had always wanted children, but he had Gemma, and that was more than enough for him. Enoch wanted to marry Gemma and build a new life with her. Enoch felt a strange sense of foreboding as he gazed at his reflection in the mirror. Fate had been cruel to both Gemma and Enoch. Fate had also brought them together. Was this happiness to last? Or did fate have some further twists to deliver?

Enoch walked across the hardwood floor of his bedroom on the fourth floor of his house. Everything around him was beautiful. The white walls and white crown molding reflected the pale white light given off by the wall lamps. Enoch didn't care for clutter. The rooms in the house in Marble Arch had very little furniture; some of the rooms were completely empty.

Gemma liked antiques, but she couldn't only afford to buy any. When she moved into her flat she had instead used the few inexpensive pieces of modern furniture that her studio flat had come with it. She had purchased a few pieces of inexpensive modern furniture for her small country house. Gemma had never asked him for money. Enoch had wanted to transfer money to her bank account, but Gemma had refused. After they married, Gemma would have access to all the money she wanted. The irony was that Gemma had never really wanted money; she had only wanted to love and be loved. Why had God made her wait so long to find it? What purpose had that served? Gemma had suffered. Enoch wasn't sure exactly what she had gone through, but he knew it must have been horrible. Enoch was blessed to have Gemma; a good-hearted person who loved him for him and only wanted to spend what remined of her life with him. Gemma had been deeply scarred by so many people.

Enoch looked out the window of the house. It was snowing. The street and park were covered in snow. Enoch looked carefully at his silver Omega watch: 9:01am. He had a long day in the trenches ahead of him.

Enoch picked up his encrypted smartphone. He tapped out something on the screen, and ten seconds later a message appeared. The driver was already waiting downstairs for him. The security team would shadow him to the office.

Last night he had met the leader of the highly secretive second team. The news was not good.

Yes, a new group was now testing the defenses. The Spaniard had all of his top people looking into it. Yes, the retired soldier was concerned. This time it was different. Whoever was leading the other security group was extremely able and undoubtably dangerous. No one went to these lengths unless violence was in the offing.

The Spaniard was aggressive. He would hunt down these people quickly. Of course, there would be violence. Enoch never asked about that aspect of the team's operations. He left it to its commanders to decide the best course of action. And a large part of Enoch did not want to know what they did in order to protect him. They did what they had to do.

Enoch paid them all well and gave them access to large amounts of cash via disconnected (untraceable) secret bank accounts. Enoch understood that the world was not a safe place—not anymore. Civilization had been fraying around the edges for decades; now everything was on the verge of coming undone.

Enoch truly wished that he could retire and live in peace and seclusion with Gemma in the Lake District. How he wished that were still possible. It was not. No one was safe anymore. No one.

Gemma—The Carthage Option—The Orta

LONDON

The Revenant accelerated as the dark blue car maneuvered through the late afternoon traffic. Late afternoon in the winter in London meant nightfall. The dark blue Peugeot's headlights cut through the darkness. The traffic in this part of London wasn't as heavy as other parts of the city. However, London was not the driver's final destination this afternoon. He was on his way to meet an old friend.

SURREY

The small village was located on the banks of a river. It was made up of small cottages, semi-detached houses, a stone Medieval church (which had replaced an Anglo-Saxon one), a post office, two pubs, a book store, and manor house which now housed a CofE infant and nursery school with 'outstanding academic results' (Ofsted) for the well-heeled families that resided here. The village had no less than 37 listed buildings in it—most of which were centuries years old. Most of the village residents commuted to London.

The village was a quiet place, a very English place. The heavily forested village consisted of only four cobblestone streets with an ancient Roman stone fountain in the middle of it all. The village breathed the ancient. The trees which lined the streets were at least a hundred years old. The village was hidden; shrouded behind a dense forest of tall trees. The village was bypassed by the A25. That was for the best. Most urbanites would drive by the village unaware that one even existed on the other side of the forest. That was by design.

Today, a foreigner, an interloper, an immigrant from a country that no longer existed, would enter the village via the single lane road that snaked through the snow-clad forest. The Revenant had an appointment with a local. Yes, it was here, just an hour away from London, that an extremely dangerous Englishman lived.

THE JANISSARY

Jem was an unusual man. He stood six feet tall and had a solid, muscular, if slender frame. He had joined the British Paras at 17, served for three years, and had been court-martialed, jailed (which included hard labor) and upon completion of his prison term, expelled from the British army. He then joined the French Foreign Legion at the age of 22.

Jem was a warrior, a true soldier. Jem was extremely self-disciplined—when he felt like it. Yes, he often chaffed under orders, but only ones that were given by incompetent officers. And there were a lot them.

Jem was brutal and prone to violence. It wasn't that he enjoyed violence; he didn't. But the world, being the way it is, required violence if one were to get anything done. Jem had enjoyed his time in the Legion. He didn't like everyone in its ranks, but he liked enough of the other legionaries to get promoted to corporal. And then the wars in Yugoslavia changed everything.

All true soldiers want to see action. Dozens, if not eventually hundreds of

Legionnaires, left the Legion to fight in the Yugoslav Civil Wars. Jem was one of them. Jem fought against Serbia and Montenegro for years in Croatia and Bosnia.

Eventually the battle hardened Jem left the former Yugoslavia and made his way east to the ex-Soviet Union, ~~like so many others~~ like a very small number of his comrades. He also fought in wars in other places beyond Europe, but let's not get ahead of ourselves.

To fight on one of the losing sides of the wars in the Former Yugoslavia and the ex-Soviet Union, marked one for a very different future. Whether that future was good or bad did not really matter. The point is this: You fought in those wars voluntarily because you were different from everyone else. Those wars had changed you, in both good and bad ways, but they had changed you. No one understood you, not even people who had served in other armies in other wars. When you fought against the Serbs, Montenegrins, and Russians, you were fighting heavily armed, relatively modern armies with little more than a rifle and a few dozen bullets. If you were really lucky, you would have a helmet. Virtually every piece of equipment, including weapons and bullets would have been taken off the corpses of your enemies. Or your friends. There were no army depots issuing machine guns and bullets to you. And if you were wounded, there might not even be a medic to treat your wounds. You would most likely bleed out and die, like so many of comrades had before your very eyes.

All of this changed you.

You could not identify with people who had served in well-equipped armies. You couldn't begin to explain what it was like to fight in an army which offered almost nothing—but a good cause. It was only the knowledge that you were fighting evil that made life in the trenches bearable for you. How you hated those who sneered at you for volunteering for a lost cause. What utter cowards these people were. **Who were they to judge you or anyone else?**

These were the same people who had done nothing while their homelands sank into ruin. They were content to play while civilization collapsed around them.

But you were different.

You had seen and experienced how cold and dark the world really was. You had experienced what is what like to have **a country annihilated around you** and disappear forever. And you knew that eventually that darkness would envelop the world. Many of you broke down. You couldn't live with the despair. You are not weak, but there was no one to guide you out of the emptiness that awaited you at home. You were alone because you knew that no one there would ever understand you. And after a while, you no longer cared if any of them did.

Now you were free.

Jem was free. The Revenant was not. **Not yet.**

THE ANGLICAN CHURCH
The Revenant, in faded blue jeans, a white button-down Oxford dress shirt, a dark wool grey v-neck jumper, a dark blue duffle coat, and brown leather Chelsea boots, entered the church, which had been constructed of ironstone rubble with sandstone buttresses, through a set of large wooden double doors. The interior was dimly lit by wall mounted lamps (most of which had been switched off). The two rows of wooden pews were empty. The stone altar, which was illuminated in shadowy light, stood bare.

The church appeared to be empty. But it wasn't. The Revenant knew that. Jem was here. Somewhere.

'I'm over here, mate,' said a male voice. Jem's voice was not deep, nor harsh. Jem spoke in a West Country dialect, the dialect closest to the old British language of the Anglo-Saxons, which was rooted in Germanic languages.

The Revenant looked in the direction of the voice—which was behind him. Yes, Jem was one of the few people in the world that had the ability to approach the Revenant unnoticed.

Jem was in his early fifties. He was handsome. In another life, he could have been an actor or even a male model, if such a thing had interested him. It hadn't in this life.

He walked from behind a medieval stone pillar and stood next to one of the pews. Jem, clad in dark khaki wool trousers, a white dress shirt, and a navy blue wool dress coat, motioned form the Revenant to join him in a darkened corner of the church. Jem had placed two wooden chairs in the corner that afternoon.

The Revenant sat down next to Jem.

'Don't worry. No one ever comes in here on weekdays. The cleaner locks the place up at 10pm. We won't be bothered until then,' said Jem quietly looking at his watch.

'How have you been?' asked the Revenant in his accented English.

'Bored. And you?'

'Busy,' replied the Revenant.

'I have assembled the team that you requested. All of them ready and awaiting orders,' said Jem.

'Good. I knew I could rely on you.'

The Revenant looked around the church. Yes, there were Latin words inscribed on the walls. But the Revenant didn't understand Latin. He looked back at Jem.

'Did you ever encounter a Spaniard from Ceuta who had served in the Spanish Foreign Legion?' asked the Revenant.

'Yes. Several. At least three that I can think of off the top of my head,' replied Jem.

'Did any of them speak Arabic fluently?'

'I don't know how fluent they were, but they all spoke some. Why do you ask?' asked Jem quietly.

'A Spaniard from Ceuta is leading a security team that I am trying to learn more about. He would be in early fifties. Also, he may have light brown hair, but I'm not sure. I know he speaks at least four languages. And he is now in England, somewhere.'

'Who is he providing security for?'

The Revenant need not mention to Jem that the contents of the conversation remain a secret. Jem understood that.

'Enoch Tara.'

'Who is that?' asked Jem.

'A billionaire in the City. My client is interested in him. But he is well protected, when he chooses to be.'

'What do you mean?' asked Jem quietly.

'Tara sometimes goes without security. Completely unprotected. Tara has one official security team and one unofficial one that is off the books. These teams have little, if any contact at all, with each other. The second unit is highly secretive. I know very little about it. I know the leader is a Spaniard who served in the Spanish Foreign Legion. I need to know the identity of the Spaniard,' said the Revenant.

'**We live in a very small world.** Why haven't I heard of any these people?' asked Jem.

'Because they are good at what they do. Because they have discipline.

Because their leader is a worthy one,' said the Revenant.

Jem leaned back in the wooden pew. He was quiet for a moment, deep in thought. Reflective. The Revenant let him think. Perhaps Jem would come up with some useful information or insight. Jem was not well educated, but he was intelligent and highly cunning. And Jem had lived a real life, an interesting, if chaotic, life. And with that unusual life came wisdom. Jem understood the parallel world that they inhabited: The world of the **security echelon. The line of iron** that separated their clients (whether good or evil) from the teeming, ignorant, and emotional masses.

'If there are Spanish Legionnaires in England, they shouldn't be too difficult to locate. Do you have a database on former and serving members of the Spanish Foreign Legion?' asked Jem.

'No. But I am trying to get one.'

'Then you will also need to access immigration. If he is using his real name, he will be there. Look for the people whose names, ages, and addresses best match the names on the Spanish army database. The list should be a short one. Then look for people who live in London. And then the people who have any connection to one of the Tara's companies. I doubt that would work for the leader of this unit, but it might work for some of his subordinates. If you can detect any Spanish employees working for Tara in any capacity, that will be a lead,' said Jem quietly.

'I had thought of doing something like that, but I don't have the connections. I can probably get hold of a list former Spanish Legionnaires, but I don't have any connections like that in the British government that would give me access to government databases. Do you?'

'No. I don't. What about your employer?' asked Jem.

'I'm sure he does. He must. I will see what I can do. But my employer can be reckless. I would rather not involve him directly in this. His side of the project is filled with too many unreliable people. I'm almost certain there would be a leak. And if the information did leak out, then the Spaniard's unit would react,' said the Revenant quietly.

'What is the end game with this Spaniard?'

'I don't know yet,' said the Revenant.

Jem looked at the Revenant for a moment. Jem's face was like stone.

'After this assignment, if I am still alive, I am going to retire. I will have more money than I need. My mother is old and frail. I have put her through a lot. I am ashamed of it. I should have spent more time with her when she was younger and healthier. God blessed me with a good mother, and I have taken her for granted. I am trying to make up for that now. I could lose her at any moment. It really bothers me. After this, I'll return to this village and stay with her in our cottage. We live near the water. I asked my mother a few months ago if I had been a disappointment to her. She said I had never disappointed her. Even when I ended up at hard labor, she said she understood the situation, and that I was right to do what I did. My mother said that she had always been proud of me. All I feel whenever I think about how I have treated her is regret and shame. I want to make it up to her,' said Jem quietly.

'It's not too late. You have a chance. Your mother is still here with you. Mine isn't,' said the Revenant quietly.

Jem didn't ask any questions about the Revenant's mother. He didn't know what her fate had been, and with the few horrible details of the Revenant's life that Jem did know, he didn't want to know anymore. Suddenly, Jem felt guilty for mentioning his mother in the Revenant's presence.

The Revenant could sense that. He didn't ever want a good person to feel bad about mentioning a loved one in a kind way in front of him. It wasn't the fault of the good that he had lost his family.

'Your mother is blessed to have a son like you, Jem.'

Gemma—The Carthage Option—The Riley

MERCIA

The black 1956 Riley Pathfinder had been a wedding gift to the 21st Baron from his wealthy in-laws. The 21st Baron and his wife had had a happy life together. His son, Wren's grandfather, the 22nd Baron, had only happy memories of his parents. When his father passed away, his mother drove it every day. The Riley reminded her of her husband and it was comforting for her to motor it through the village or to London to see her parents. The 22nd Baron usually accompanied her. And when, eight years later, on a warm summer day in July, his mother, the baroness, passed away, he continued to drive the old car because it reminded him of his parents.

Wren remembered her grandfather well. The former Coldstream Guards officer was intelligent and wise. He told Wren of the importance of family and the how important it was to appreciate her parents while they were with her, for one day, they would not be, and Wren would miss them terribly. Wren had been grateful that she had had that conversation with her grandfather. The financial struggles of the family had taken a deep toll on them all, but Wren never failed to tell her parents how much she loved them.

After her grandfather had passed away, her father's army postings had taken them away from the manor house, sometimes for a year at a time. The Riley, parked in the Georgian coach house, had started to decay. One day, it stopped running. A few months later, the tires had gone flat. And one day the Riley was covered with a white tarp and forgotten. They family didn't have the money to repair it. It was allowed to sit in the cold dark cart shed next to the Thornycroft—for years.

It was the sale of the 1953 Big Ben Thornycroft that allowed the family to repair the Riley. Wren's father searched the Internet until he found a garage with the necessary spare parts and skills to do it. The garage was an hour away from the manor house, and the owner, a Riley enthusiast, drove out to have a look at the car himself. The owner had the Riley towed back to the garage. He had the Riley running within two days. He worked alongside the other mechanics who repaired the brakes, changed the tires, along with some electrical work. Yes, the car, overall, was in remarkably good condition. After a week of repairs, the Riley was mechanically sound. Now all the car needed was a new leather interior and a new coat of paint.

THE RILEY

Wren sat in the front seat of the car; Freya, Wallis, and Jinx sat together in the large leather bench seat (that could comfortably seat three) in the back. The Riley's smooth, streamlined body had two fog lights on either side of the large distinctive thick-rimmed curving vertical grill which was topped with the glossy blue Riley badge. The Riley had chrome hubcaps and chrome headlamp rims. In the center of each tire was the Riley chrome hubcap badge. The car was rounded out with a sweeping tail. The walnut dash was set with three large Smith's dials. The interior had been upholstered in beige leather. The steering wheel, in set with a semi-circular ring which control the direction indicators, was huge and looked like something taken from an Art Deco art exhibit.

The beige leather seats were worn and cracked in places, but, 'I'm having the interior reupholstered next week. I'm also going to have the car repainted too,' said the baron happily as he piloted the giant four-door saloon car through the snow.

The car smelled of leather and wood. The engine ran smoothly. The Riley had a Borg-Warner overdrive automatic transmission, a rare, but original option offered in 1956. The car glided through the small village quietly. Outside the windows, people could be seen shoveling snow, walking through the village carrying groceries, or entering the village pub. The baron pushed a button and the heater came on. It worked well.

'Yes, they even managed to repair the heater.'

Freya looked at her watch: 3:25pm. It would be dark in an hour. The day had been an interesting one for Freya. She liked Wren. Wren was still unpopular at Muddy Hills, but hopefully that would change. Freya felt a new affinity towards people like Rex, Wren, and Jinx. They were Rhodesian, or half-Rhodesian. They knew the life of an exile, a refugee. And unlike other refugees, Rhodesians were looked upon as unworthy of any sympathy at all by many. That was truly horrible.

'Yes, Wren, the car runs well. I never thought it would it run again, but I am glad that it is. After it is painted, it will become my daily driver,' said the baron.

THE MANOR HOUSE

After the girls returned to the house, they all took a quick shower (well, Wallis took a long one). The girls changed into warm wool jumpers, white cotton blouses, and dark khaki cotton trousers, except for Wallis, who wore a pair of dark blue wool trousers. The fortified manor house was drafty. The hallways and entry hall were unheated. Wren's bedroom, was, at the moment, unheated too.

THE BEDROOM

This is my room,' said Wren as she opened the wide glossy white door. The white walled room was down the hall on the second floor of the house. It was smaller than the room the girls were staying in, but it had a much better view. The long wood plank floors creaked with every step.

'Don't worry, you won't fall through.'

Wren had a four-poster bed. The bed was made of oak. The bed had an ornately carved backboard and tester from which had been hung with curtains made of tapestry. The four thick wooden posters were carved with heraldic decoration.

'The bed looks Medieval, but it is actually Victorian. The tapestry hangings are reproductions of a tapestry that used to hang in the great hall downstairs. Yes, the mattress is new. It's from Finland. It's *quite* comfortable. The white sheets are Egyptian cotton,' said Wren.

On the opposite wall was a limestone fireplace with an antique carved oak Jacobean overmantel. The room, like the other rooms of the manor house, was a mix of centuries of English style. The walls were covered in a fresh coat of white paint.

'Now that the ceiling has been repaired, I plan to hang wallpaper in my room this spring,' said Wren.

'This room is fantastic, Wren,' said Jinx. 'I feel like I am on a movie set.'

'Thank you, Jinx. Yes, I really like my room. Originally the walls were oak

Tudor panels, the wallpaper came later. The constant water damage made hanging wallpaper impossible, but now I have the option,' said Wren.

On the opposite wall of the room was a wooden wardrobe. There was a small wooden desk next to the window with two wooden chairs. Several books were stacked on it next to a table lamp. There was also a narrow wooden bookshelf, next to one of the windows, with dozens of books in it.

'I plan to hang some photos and a painting on the walls this spring too. Now I can decorate my room as I wish.'

At that moment, a ray of orange light illuminated Wren. The girls all turned and looked out the window; outside, the sun was disappearing quickly.

Wren smiled.

'What would you like to do tonight?' asked Wren.

'Stay warm,' said Wallis. 'Beyond that, I'm up for almost anything.'

Outside, the house and grounds were blanketed in snow and ice. The temperature was dropping by the minute. The thick forest of trees, mostly bereft of leaves, swayed in the icy winds.

'Yes, I think a night in is in order,' said Wren happily. 'How about pizza?'

'*Okay, yah!*' replied Jinx happily.

'I love pizza,' said Freya.

'Me, too,' said Wallis.

'I told Mummy earlier that we would probably be having pizza. There is a rather good Italian restaurant in the village. The owner used to work at the best restaurants and hotels in London. Now she has returned to the village and runs a restaurant. She also makes great lasagna.'

Freya arched an eyebrow. 'Lasagna is my *fav*,' said Freya.

'Alright, then we will order pizza and lasagna,' said Wren.

'Wren, you and your parents have been gracious hosts. Please, please. Let me the buy tonight's dinner. I insist,' said Freya.

'No. You are our guests. The lord and future lord of the manor will buy you pizza and lasagna,' said Wren and she smiled.

'Please, Wren,' said Jinx. 'Let a fellow Rhodesian pay for dinner. I rarely get the opportunity to speak with someone from Bulawayo.'

'Yes, Wren. As a future baroness with a ruined castle of my own, I would like to contribute to tonight's feast.'

'Oh, thank you, girls. You are very kind,' answered Wren. 'But you are my guests.'

'Wren, we didn't bring anything for the hosts. We should have,' said Freya.

'It's a small thing, but it would mean a lot to us,' said Jinx.

Wren thought about it for a moment. And a moment more.

'Oh, come on, Wren. Let us do this small thing for you and your parents. I want to buy dinner too,' said Wallis in her Sloaney intonation.

Wren smiled. 'Alright, girls. Thank you.'

Wallis smiled and said, 'Alright, well then, let's add pasta and garlic bread to the order.'

And everybody laughed.

TO THE MANOR BORN

The drawing room, once the great hall of the manor house, was now a gloriously Jacobean room. Its white plaster Jacobean ceiling was beautiful, glorious, and English. The long plank wooden floor, once covered by an antique rug from Persia, was now bare wood. The freshly painted white walls were welcoming. The large white marble chimneypiece, which covered half the wall and touched the ceiling of the room, was ornately carved with Jacobean patterns and the family's coat of arms. The marble fireplace glowed and crackled with warmth. A 17th century grandfather clock ticked quietly next to one of the double doors to the drawing room. The sound of the clock was soothing and almost reassuring.

There were two sofas and five upholstered armchairs, all but one was from the 1920s. The furniture had ben upholstered in dark blue velvet (with white piping) in 1979; the year Margaret Thatcher had become Prime Minister and saved England from complete ruin. In 1999, the 22nd Baron had them reupholstered with the same fabric. Two of the armchairs were upholstered in the same dark blue fabric of the sofas.

One large armchair was upholstered in buffalo leather, a gift from one of the 22nd Baron's American friends who had large ranch (and oil wells) in Texas. The chair was now placed near the large window that looked out on the lawn and trees behind the house. It was a happy and poignant reminder of Wren's beloved grandfather. The remaining armchair had been reupholstered for Wren by her mother, the baroness, for her 17th birthday. Wren had been having a difficult time at her boarding school and her mother had wanted to cheer her up. The baroness had saved money from her job working at a bakery while the 23rd Baron was posted in Surrey. Wren's mother had purchased the expensive fabric from a high-end shop in London recommended to her by a friend. The fabric had vibrant purple lavenders, bright red poppies, and purple Michaelmas daisies woven onto a white background. Wren loved all things Jane Austen, and her mother hoped that her unhappy daughter would like it. She did. She loved the reupholstered chair. It was Wren's. And she sat in it whenever she spent time in the drawing room with her family.

On one wall of the drawing room was a gilt framed Elizabethan portrait of one of the baron's ancestors. The ancestor of the 23rd Baron had been handsome. The oil painting showed a man with his neck hidden behind a large white ruff collar. The dark bluish black background was decorated with arcane symbols and Latin words. The Elizabethans liked secrecy and were obsessed with mysterious symbols and codes. The 16th century baron's image was surrounded by an array of symbols, figures, inscriptions and arcane imagery. The baron, baroness, and Wren knew what all the symbols meant. They were one of the family's secrets. The painting was also one of the few works of art the family had retained.

The baron loved spending time with his family. His foreign assignments had meant being separated from his family for a year at a time. When he did return, Wren was usually away at boarding school. Finally, after decades of financial struggle, God had granted the family a moment of peace. The sale of the Thornycroft had given them enough money to repair the roof and the old Riley. The baron had sold his Toyota when he retired three years ago. He needed the money to make repairs to the house. The baroness's hatchback had been their sole vehicle. The baron once again had savings in addition to his army pension. A feeling of tranquility had descended upon the family—finally.

The future of the family pile was far from secure. However, the baron had decided that that worry was best left to the future. Wren, gorgeous in white and pale blue paisley pyjamas and a pair of blue velvet slippers, entered the drawing room on the first floor of the house. It had been a cold walk down the marble staircase. Wren, her long honey blonde hair over one shoulder and her bangs partially covering her eyes, smiled when she saw her parents, both in country tweeds, sitting together on a sofa.

'The girls would like to buy us pizza tonight. They have all insisted. They wanted to do something to thank us for hosting them this weekend. We've all had a nice time. Thank you, Mummy. Thank you, Daddy. I know you have worked hard to make it all possible.

Wren's parents were quite moved; not only by the kind gesture of the girls, but by Wren's obvious happiness. 'That's very nice of them,' said the baron.

'Yes, very sweet. Such nice girls. I'm glad you have friends like this, Wren, said the baroness.

Wren smiled. 'What kind of pizza would you like? We are going to order one just for you.'

'I'll have what your having,' said the baron while looking at the baroness. 'Pepperoni and pineapple,' said the baroness. 'Thin crust.'

THE ROOM UPSTAIRS
'Yes, three large thin crust pizzas. Two Hawaiian and one pepperoni...Yes, one large order of lasnaga and four pieces of garlic bread,' said Wren into her smartphone. 'Yes. Thank you...The name is Wren Talbot...Yes. The baron's daughter. You know where I live then...Thank you.'

Wren tapped the glowing screen of her phone and looked up. 'The pizza should be here within the hour.'

The girls had all changed into pyjamas. Freya was lying flat on her back on top of her camp bed. The folding metal bed was surprisingly comfortable. Her blonde hair covered most of the soft white pillow. Freya was sore and tired after the long day in the frozen ruins, but she was glad that she had had the chance to explore the castle ruins with the others.

Ping.

Freya's smartphone glowed upon receiving the text. It was from Louise.

It's freezing here in London. A lot of snow. Aurelia and I are studying for exams. I will be so glad when this term is over. How are you, Freya?

Freya smiled and tapped out a text message on her phone.

At Wren's country house with Jinx and another friend named Wallis. Toured a ruined castle today with a secret tunnel. Nearly froze to death. We have ordered pizza and lasagna. And pasta and garlic bread. How was the kale in the student cafeteria today? :)

Ping.

Who's Wren? And no, we didn't eat kale. Today I had a boiled potato and Aurelia ate apple slices in the cafeteria. Pizza?! I wish I were there, Freya.

Freya suddenly felt guilty.

Wren is a girl you lives down the hall from me at Muddy Hills. I'll buy you Hawaiian pizza during the Christmas holidays. The family has invited you to stay with us in Mayfair. Please, say yes, Louise. Afterwards we will visit Poppy and then take the train to Northumberland to see my grandparents. I will buy you pizza at a restaurant in the village near the house in Northumberland. It's really good.

Ping.

Thank you for inviting me. Please tell your family how grateful I am. Yes, I would love to spend Christmas with you and your family, Freya. I miss you.

Freya felt a tinge of sadness as she read Louise's text. Yes, fate had separated them this year, but next year they would both be attending the gloriously unwoke Midlands-Hasegawa university together. Then all would be well.

I miss you, too, Louise. See you soon.

Gemma—The Carthage Option—Marble Arch

LONDON

The silver Volvo S60 inched forward slowly. It was 8:29pm. The other automobiles in either lane of traffic illuminated the car in the ultra-bright white halogen light of the headlamps and the red glow of the tail lights. The Volvo's glossy polar silver paint reflected and redirected the light onto other cars.

It had stopped snowing just an hour earlier. A thin layer of snow now covered London. The sky was pitch black; the Moon concealed behind the clouds.

Enoch Tara, in a dark grey wool suit, white dress shirt, and a red, dark blue, and grey tartan tie, sat in the back of the car deep in thought. He did not pay attention to his surroundings. He paid others to do that for him.

The suit and booted driver, his brown hair cut like a City Banker, scanned the traffic ahead. The blond, athletic man in faded jeans, a black mock turtle neck, and black leather Chelsea boots, seated in the front passenger seat, careful noted everything and everyone in the vicinity of the car. Two car lengths behind them was a black Audi A6. The two men in that vehicle were also part of Enoch Tara's security detail.

The situation had changed.

The Spaniard, a retired soldier of the Spanish Foreign Legion and the leader of Enoch Tara's secretive security unit, had warned him an hour before in the starkest of terms of the very real danger Enoch now faced. An unknown enemy was now stalking the Spaniard's supposedly secretive security team. How was that possible? Secrecy had always been paramount. This group had operated (apparently) undetected for years. How had that information gotten out? **Who had talked?** And more importantly: Who were the people following Tara's special security unit and why were they doing it?

Enoch Tara wondered if the same people behind the market disruptions were also attempting to move against him personally. Tara's financial empire had remained invincible behind an impregnable fortress of absolute security and Enoch's own Jupiterian discernment and unrivalled financial abilities. Yes, Enoch had detected moves being made against him, but he been able to counter them. The trail to the perpetrators, however, had remained cold. Perhaps this was an entirely different group of people? Or, perhaps, it was the same people shaking the financial world? If that was the case, then Enoch Tara was in real trouble. Yes, violence would be in the offing.

It had never occurred to Enoch that he would not be the intended victim. Enoch had always assumed from the beginning that it would be him. The Spaniard had agreed. That someone else could fall prey to the unknown enemy had never even crossed Enoch's mind.

THE STUDIO FLAT

Gemma looked into the mirror again; this time more carefully. Yes, there were more white, silver, and grey hairs. Gemma never attempted to remove or conceal her gradually greying hair. She wasn't worried about it marring her appearance. Getting old was inevitable. Gemma was grateful that she had survived all she had and had found someone who truly loved her, grey hair or not.

Gemma titled her head one way and then another. She tilted her head to the right. Her complexion was clear, glowing. A healthy diet and regular exercise had kept her toned and healthy.

Gemma straightened out her white cotton blouse, her platinum and diamond engagement ring sparkling and flashing as she did so. Gemma was wearing a pair of faded blue jeans tonight. Gemma loved wearing blue jeans when not at work. Blue jeans liberated her. Perhaps it was the Americanism of them that did it? Yes, America, so free of the rigidness of England. Gemma smiled.

Gemma stepped out of the small white tiled bathroom and closed the door. The small flat was enclosed in white walls and illuminated by a modern light fixture that was suspended above the kitchen table. Gemma had carefully set the table for two. A white table cloth set with two white porcelain plates, inexpensive silverware, glasses, and (carefully folded) white cotton napkins. Gemma had used a clear plastic ruler to ensure things had been placed correctly.

Gemma had made dinner for two. Enoch hadn't been eating much lately. He had looked rather thin the last time they had met for lunch. Steak was in order. So was a fresh green salad. Gemma was worried about him.

Gemma looked out the window of her flat; it was starting to snow. She looked at her silver Cartier watch: 9:03pm.

The electronic door bell sounded. Gemma walked across the room and looked into the CCTV monitor. It was Enoch and a muscular and menacing blond man were standing outside the main door of the apartment building.

Gemma buzzed them in.

THE FLAT
After Enoch had entered Gemma's flat (along with a burst of cold air from the unheated hallway), the towering bodyguard went back to the elevator and went back downstairs. No doubt the security team would wait for Enoch downstairs in their vehicles.

Gemma had grown used to security teams in the last year. Violet always travelled with security when in London now, so did Freya. Brian had installed a security system in Poppy's semi-detached along with reinforced doors and shutters. Külli had installed a panic room in her house in Marble Arch. The old London was gone, and it was never coming back. London had changed forever.

Gemma helped Enoch take off his dark grey wool overcoat. She carefully hung Enoch's overcoat on a wooden peg near the front door to her flat. Enoch put on a pair of white slippers that Gemma kept for guests in front of the door.

'You looked exhausted,' said Gemma as she poured cold water from a plastic bottle in her silver SMEG refrigerator into a tall glass. She handed it to Enoch. Enoch smiled faintly and drank it slowly.

'Thank you, Gem. It's been a long day at the office.'

'Why not lay down for a while?' asked Gemma.

'You don't mind?' asked Enoch quietly.

'No.'

Gemma led Enoch over to her bed, which was covered with a large white duvet, and helped Enoch take off his dark grey blazer and sit down on the bed. The slender 5' 9" Enoch seemed even smaller at that moment.

'Lay down. I have to finish preparing dinner. I'll wake you when its ready.'

'Thank you, Gem.'

Gemma turned around and walked to the closet and hung Enoch's dark grey jacket on a wooden hanger. She then walked back to the stainless steel kitchen counter. She refilled the glass with water and then walked back to Enoch. She had been gone less than a minute, Enoch was already asleep on top of Gemma's bed, sunk into the white duvet.

Gemma carefully removed the white slippers and then gently lifted his legs up onto the bed and turned him at an angle so he fit onto the bed completely. She covered him with a navy blue wool blanket. She let him sleep.

Gemma—The Carthage Option—The Apartment

LONDON

Enoch opened his eyes. It was dark. A narrow shaft of light (from a crack in the curtains) dimly illuminated the room. Everything was in shadows. He was lying in bed. Outside he could hear a car moving down the street. He looked around. He wasn't at home. He was in Gemma's flat. What time was it? He had arrived at Gemma's for dinner and fallen asleep. Where was Gemma? Enoch turned his head an could see Gemma's slim body lying next to him under a wool blanket. She was breathing gently.

Enoch was in bed with Gemma.

Enoch and Gemma had never shared a bed until that moment. Gemma had remained chaste. Enoch was not surprised. They hadn't married yet. Gemma was a proper woman. It was only natural (for Gemma) that she behave this way. It had never bothered Enoch. He would have been disappointed if she had slept with him upon their engagement. What this meant was that Gemma trusted Enoch. She loved and trusted him. She felt safe with him. Then Enoch felt a sudden rush of urgency. What time was it?

Enoch noticed the blue glow of the digital alarm clock on top of Gemma's bookshelf: 4:05am.

Wow.

THE CITY NEVER SLEEPS

Enoch had been asleep for several hours. Enoch had needed the sleep, however, Enoch needed to see what was going on in the outside world. He felt around in the dark. Ah, there it was. Enoch picked up his encrypted smartphone and tapped on the screen: Fifty-two new messages. Fifty-two.

Enoch laid back in bed. He looked at the sleeping Gemma. Enoch never would have imagined himself here with Gemma a year ago. **It was amazing how much a person's life can change in a year.**

'Enoch? Are you awake?' said Gemma quietly as she lifted up her head and looked in his direction. Enoch was lying flat on his back in the darkness.

'Yes, Gem. I woke up a few minutes ago.'

'I thought it was best to let you sleep. How do you feel now?' asked Gemma quietly. Gemma, clad in a white t-shirt and a pair of flannel pyjama bottoms, sat up in bed. She was a slender shadowy form.

'Thank you, Gem. I feel much better.'

'You missed dinner. Are you hungry?' asked Gemma quietly.

'Yes. Are you?'

'Famished,' replied Gemma.

Gemma got out of bed. She moved through the shadowy darkness and opened the curtain just enough to allow in more light from the street lamps. Gemma stood illuminated in light. She was shapely and slender at the same time. Gemma was beautiful. Gemma smiled. She was radiantly beautiful. And she loved him.

'Would you like to take a shower? asked Gemma.

'Would that be alright?'

'Yes. I have a new bathrobe and a pair of pyjamas that I ordered for you in the closet. I was going to give them for you for Christmas, but you can have them now,' said Gemma and she smiled.

Enoch smiled.

'Thank you, Gem.'

Enoch slowly climbed out of bed. He was still fully dressed. His clothes were wrinkled. That was alright. Enoch walked across the small flat and opened the door to the tiled bathroom; he turned on the light. His eyes adjusted to the fluorescent lamps in the bathroom for a moment and then entered and closed the door behind him.

THE KITCHEN

Enoch, his brown hair still damp, and in a set of blue and red tartan pyjamas a white waffle spa bathrobe, and a pair of white slippers, watched Gemma remove covered plates from the narrow silver refrigerator. It must have been after 5am. Gemma placed the dishes on the counter. The table was still set from the night before.

The pyjamas and bathrobe are really nice. Thank you, Gemma.'

'Merry Christmas, Enoch,' said Gemma and she smiled. 'I'll heat up the steak for you,' said Gemma.

'No, Gem. That's alright. I'll eat it cold. It's already been cooked. I don't mind. Let's just relax and have a nice breakfast. Or is this a late dinner?'

'It's would ever you would like it to be.'

Gemma placed a white porcelain plate with a steak and cold mashed potatoes on it in front of Enoch. She then went back to the counter and returned with a white porcelain bowl with a green salad. Gemma went back to the stainless steel kitchen counter and returned with her own dishes. She sat down. She looked at Enoch and smiled.

'Bon appetite.'

THE STREET

When Enoch emerged from the building, it was 6:30am. It was dark and very, very cold. Two members of the security team were waiting for him in front of the building. The team waiting for him was not the same one that had accompanied Enoch to Gemma's the night before. The security team

141

had rotated fresh men into position at 3am. The silver Volvo was idling out front with the driver. The black Audi A6 was parked on the other side of the street. Enoch had changed back into his regular clothes. He was also carrying a paper shopping bag that Gemma had given him to carry his new white waffle bathrobe and tartan pyjamas home in.

The wintery air felt good. Enoch had finally gotten some sleep and a good meal. He had spent much of the night asleep next to Gemma. And he had received some early Christmas presents. Enoch was happy. Gemma had made him happy after almost two decades of despair.

Gemma—The Carthage Option—Sunday in Mercia

THE CHURCH
The baron, baroness, Wren, and the girls had all attended church that snowy morning. The baron and his party had taken up the front box pews. The sharply attired baron and baroness had greeted and been greeted by countless villagers outside the Medieval church before and after the service. The girls had enjoyed it. The vicar was also kind, if a bit reserved.

Jinx had found it all a bit overwhelming. Here, in this church, surrounded by the stone tombs of Wren's ancestors and her family's loyal retainers, Jinx could feel the supernatural ancientness of it all. Sitting in the same box pew with the baron and his family, Jinx felt connected to the past stronger than she ever had. This is England: ancient, glorious, and good.

After the church service, the family walked down the center aisle, every parishioner nodding slightly in acknowledgment as the baron passed. The double doors of the church opened, followed by a sharp blast icy cold air and natural light. Outside, Wren and her parents spoke with some of the villagers. Wren happily introduced the girls to several of the locals. The girls found it all interesting and fun. Freya had also enjoyed the sermon.

The baron drove home in the Riley with the baroness after fifteen minutes of conversation with the locals. Wallis followed them with Wren, Freya, and Jinx in the Bristol motorcar.

The sky was blue and filled with large white clouds that floated through air. The entire village was covered in a white blanket of snow. The weekend was coming to an end. The girls would be leaving soon.

THE MANOR HOUSE

The 23rd Baron smiled. Yes, it just might work. Why hadn't the family ever truly considered it? I mean really considered it? Yes, the plan that Wren had laid out for them after church that morning in the drawing room was a great idea. Wren had given all of the credit to Freya. After all, it was her suggestion and she had talked it over with Wren the night before. Freya's maternal grandparents opened the country house in Northumberland to tours in the summers, and they made quite a bit of money off of it. If Wren's family could make just a small portion of what Poppy's or Violet's families made, they could afford to keep both the house and the castle and pay their taxes. They might even have a little money left over. Yes, the baroness agreed. It was a great idea. Wren told them that Freya would put them in touch with both the Devereux and Airey families and see what further advice they could give them. Hopefully—hopefully—the family could be saved from complete ruin.

4 THE HOLLOW MEN

Gemma—The Carthage Option—La Cagoule

LONDON

It was early in the morning. It was dark. The Moon, partially hidden behind some large clouds, shone brightly. The glossy black Range Rover, its headlamps cutting through the darkness, slowed at the corner, turned, and then rolled to a stop. The driver switched off the headlights. Carter Holland, seated in the back of the SUV, looked at his platinum wristwatch. He was ten minutes early. The driver and another member of his security team sat in the front seats of the Ranger Rover. They both took in the surroundings.

HIGHGATE CEMETERY

The blond Carter Holland, clad in a black cashmere overcoat, walked towards the cemetery wall alone. It was freezing cold; a thick layer of snow covered the ground. The snow crunched underfoot as he approached the hidden entrance to the cemetery. He heard a loud creaking sound as he walked towards the door. Someone had been waiting for him in the cold. The heavily weathered wooden door was open. A slender young man, in a dark suit, white shirt, and dark necktie, nodded slightly as he approached.

'The Baron is waiting for you in the tomb, sir,' said a young man with a Yorkshire accent.

The young man led Carter Holland through the tombstones, barren trees, and crypts. It was dark, the young man used the narrow beam of light from a small stainless steel penlight to find his way. The large trees sagged under the weight of the freshly fallen snow. It was a windless and freezing night. The men walked through the snowy cemetery until they reached the entrance to the stone catacombs. Two tall silhouettes stood in the open entrance to the granite tombs. These men belonged to the Special Unit.

LA CAGOULE

Enoch Tara had a special security team—what Tara called it, if it had a name at all, remained unknown. The Revenant had been investigating Tara's special unit for several weeks and had managed to identify some of its members. Carter Holland had been frustrated with the Revenant's reticence over the identities of the members of Tara's secret security team. Carter wasn't stupid. He could sense that the head of his core army was on to them. What the Revenant planned to do with the information remained a mystery to Carter. It was pointless to argue with the Revenant. He was very much his own man—which was both good and bad. The Revenant had been hired to led the core army in securing his future country. Carter decided that Tara's Special Unit had to be confronted by Carter's own Special Unit.

The leader of this unit, an ex-Para, was as tough as nails. He was, at 38, surprisingly young to lead such a dangerous and secretive team. He was not well educated—the man's diction and accent gave that much away immediately. He was barely literate, but that didn't really matter.

'I can read faces, mate.'

Declan had grown up hard in London; one of three boys of an alcoholic single mother. One of his brothers, Gareth, the youngest, was murdered when he was thirteen, by a Jamaican drug dealer for no reason other than the yardie had been bored and decided to shoot the first person he saw walk down the alley near his parked car.

The oldest brother, Declan, was given special leave from the Paras to attend the funeral and see to the family's affairs. He did just that. The surviving brothers avenged their brother's death by killing the yardie (who was easy to track down) along with his mother and two younger teenage brothers. The police never found the bodies of the two younger brothers, only their severed hands (which had been found scattered along a railroad track). The oldest brother's dreadlocked corpse was found in five different locations across London. His body had been badly charred and burned. Only the mother's bloated corpse, with her throat cut, had been found on the blood-soaked stairway of their council flat in Hackney.

The dreadlocked yardie had died a horrific death—after three days of torture and humiliation.

Gareth had been a good student. He had had potential that his older brothers never would. He was a true academic and a gentle soul who had never bothered anyone. So, of course, his fate had been cruel. But the fate of his murderer had been far worse—Gareth's brothers had seen to that. Whenever Declan spoke of Gareth, it was almost always in the present tense. 'Gareth is a good student. Gareth is good at history.' Declan still found it difficult to believe his youngest sibling was dead. Colin accepted it. He always spoke of Gareth in the past tense. The boys' mother could not accept it and died after a heavy drinking binge. Declan had her buried next to Gareth.

But more than vengeance, the brothers had benefitted in another entirely unexpected way: They had found a new career. The yardie had, under extreme duress, given them all of his money, drugs, and guns (including the pistol that he had used to gun down the youngest brother). The brothers were in business. They specialized in robbing and murdering drug dealers. It was a lucrative trade. And the police were more than happy to look the other way.

Declan, the eldest brother, returned to the Parachute Regiment and to combat assignments across the globe. The younger brother, Colin (always a bad lad), and only eighteen at the time, rapidly assembled a violent criminal gang. The gang specialized in violent home invasions (of gangsters' homes) in London and as far afield as Manchester. London gangland, hardened to the most violent and brutal of crimes, **trembled**.

The brothers breathed violence. **They were both pure unadulterated products of modern London.**

Declan, after 20 years in the Paras, retired at the ripe old age of 37 and set up his own security company. Or so it seemed. Declan's security company supplied security teams for oil pipelines, overseas mining operations, and cargo ships sailing through pirate infested waters. The company was an immediate success.

However, within a year, Declan was (secretly) working for Carter Holland.

The Special Unit carried out their assignments for Carter Holland with unbridled glee. The Special Unit reveled in violence and cruelty. This is what a Special Unit should be like, thought Carter Holland. Carter had rarely used the unit, but when he did, it always carried out its assignments with an unrestrained burst of violence. The unit was a strange assortment of ex-Paras, gangsters, and wayward youth.

Tonight, Carter had summoned the unit's leader for a rare meeting. Declan awaited the arrival of his employer in the icy tomb of one of the aged, white-haired baron's ancestors. He didn't have to wait long.

Carter Holland entered the dimly illuminated tomb. An electric lamp had been placed on top of the grey stone sarcophagus. Seated in a folding wooden chair near the large stone sarcophagus was the aged 11th Baron. He was wrapped in a black overcoat with a brown fur collar. The baron looked frail and sickly.

Declan wore a black Saville Row suit, white shirt, and black tie. He cut his hair like a City banker. Declan, like many Paras, was handsome. He had a glossy and *rather posh* appearance; glossy, that is, until he spoke. The working-class background revealed itself immediately and the illusion was shattered. Declan was aware of this. He spoke very little. He had taken private voice lessons with an instructor at a drama school in London, but it hadn't done him any good. Declan was what he was. At least he had tried to improve himself.

'Good morning, Mr Holland,' said Declan in his working-class accent.

Carter cringed.

Declan noticed.

Carter Holland actually liked Declan. Carter understood that people like Declan, who come from a truly tough background, a council-house environment, have a sort of bare-faced courage and a willingness to put themselves in dangerous situations of their own volition that most do not. This was a bare-faced courage that Carter Holland understood, admired, and shared. Carter had also ended up in a rough local comprehensive school—blond, blue eyed, and shunned by most of his classmates. Carter had also been forced to resort to violence to survive. Only Carter's middling middle-class family had given him options that Declan's impoverish family had not. Carter respected Declan's abilities and discipline. Declan knew that.

'Good morning, Your Lordship,' said Carter as he nodded slightly in the 11th Baron's direction. The baron covered his mouth with a gloved hand, coughed, and nodded in return.

'Good morning, Declan. I'm sure you realize, that if I have summoned you here, I have an important assignment for you.'

'Sure,' replied Declan.

'You have looked through the dossier I sent?'

'Yes.'

'And?' asked Carter.

'I am still looking for the Spaniard. I reviewed the surveillance photos taken in Corbridge. I didn't recognize anyone in the photos. However, I have a lead.'

Declan took out an encrypted smartphone and tapped on the screen. Photos started to appear.

Gemma—The Carthage Option—The Crown

ENGLAND

Her name, The Honourable Wren Elizabeth Talbot, not only denoted Wren's nobility, but was also a pledge of allegiance and loyalty to Queen Elizabeth II and the Crown. The English baronial family's loyalty was absolute and unshakable. (Or was it?) Queen Elizabeth II had reigned since 1952. Wren's family was devoted to the Monarchy. But was the Monarchy worthy of such devotion and loyalty? Had the Queen protected those who had given and would willingly give their lives to protect hers? Was the Monarchy still working in the interests of its loyal subjects? Would the Royal Family eventually betray Wren and those like her? Had the House of Windsor already betrayed them?

For Wren, England, the Monarchy, and her ancestral lands were her life. Without them, she would have no purpose, no joy, and no future. Her family was ancient and it was tied to the fate of England and the British Crown—for better **or worse.**

For Louise, her life was tied to the land, to East Anglia, where her family had lived for thousands of years. Louise loved England. The Monarchy, as an institution, was important to her. Her family had always lived under kings and queens (with the exception of the Interregnum), but different blood lines had ruled or reigned over the land. The Crown, hopefully, would be worn by someone worthy of it. Louise was loyal to her people, her ancestors, and the land. Louise was very loyal to Queen Elizabeth II and had had picture of her on the wall of her room at All Saints.

For Jinx, the Rhodesian, the ties to the Crown were tenuous, at best. The Queen had not come to the aid of Rhodesia. Queen Elizabeth II had opposed it. For Jinx, 'the Queen' meant the British monarchy, but in an abstract way. Jinx believed in monarchy; she loved England, her ancestral homeland, but she had always viewed the Queen in a cold light. For Jinx, the Crown was not tied to one family. It certainly wasn't tied to the House of Windsor (formerly the House of Saxe-Coburg and Gotha). Jinx was loyal to some of the others who had worn the English Crown. This family of Germans had betrayed Rhodesia, the Rhodesians, and her family. Jinx (Jane) hoped that one day, the Crown would rest on the head of someone worthy. For Jinx, her loyalty was to her ancestral land and people. When Jinx saluted 'the Crown', it was only to those who had worn it with unswerving loyalty to England and the English.

Jinx, like Louise, was English. Jinx was also as much Rhodesian as she was English. And Louise was as Anglo-Saxon as she was English.

Poppy was loyal to Crown and Country. Poppy was loyal to Queen Elizabeth II. However, Poppy felt, like Jinx, that the Crown was not the sole remit of a single family. The Devereux family had an almost mystical regard for the Monarchy; however, several royal families had held the Crown, some much more worthy of it than others. That England, the English, and the Crown survive were the family priorities. But above all, England and the English people must survive. With or without a monarchy, England must survive.

Külli, the only child of Estonian refugees, felt two things when she thought of England: gratitude and British. Gratitude that England had taken in her family. The Vahtras had, through strenuous effort, become wealthy entrepreneurs and British. They were extremely loyal to the Queen. The family had built a successful business. The Vahtras paid their taxes, were law-abiding, Külli's father had served in the British army (National Service), and he had restored a modest English country house. Külli had been sent to one of England's premier boarding schools and become a true British girl. (At least that's how Külli's parents had viewed it.) Külli was a credit to England, her parents' adopted homeland. The Vahtras were loyal to England. That is as it should be. An immigrant and the children of immigrants, should behave like a guest in someone's else home. Gratitude and loyalty were important.

For The Honourable Gemma Ophelia Ripley, England was her love and life. Gemma was ardent monarchist; however, it was to Baroness Thatcher of Kesteven, not Queen Elizabeth II, that Gemma looked to for guidance and inspiration. It was Margaret Hilda Thatcher's photos that had adorned the walls of Gemma's rooms at Somerville College, Oxford, not the Queen's. (Somerville was a formerly all-girl college that Margaret Thatcher had tried to keep all-girl.) Gemma loved England and the English. Gemma was not, and never would be, British. Gemma was English. Gemma's loyalty was to the English and England.

Freya had always had a different take on the situation. Freya was English. She was part of an ancient family that could trace its lineage back to the ancient Northumbrians. She was a member of the nobility; several noble bloodlines coursed through her veins. And yet, Freya's true loves were her family and friends. Freya loved England, but the England that her mother had grown up in had already vanished. Why should Freya tie her fate to a place that no longer existed? Freya's father, Hugh, had been born in Rhodesia; the product of an English father and Rhodesian mother. He had borne witness to the events there and had decided that he would not allow Violet and Freya to go through in England what he had been through in Rhodesia. Freya's father had decided to leave England. Of course, Violet would not agree to go until both of her parents had passed away, but Hugh knew that once they had departed this world, Violet would consent to leave England forever. Freya had decided to become a flight attendant while at All Saints, which would be a good way to explore the world and find a new home. Freya would take Louise with her—if Louise would go. Freya prayed that Louise would agree to leave too.

Gemma—The Carthage Option—The Residence Halls

THE MIDLANDS
The girls, that is, Freya, Jinx, Wallis, and Wren, returned to wintery Midlands-Hasegawa University on Sunday evening to find that the boilers had still not been repaired. Muddy Hills faced another week of freezing temperatures and bursting water pipes. Privately, Freya was happy about it. She enjoyed camping out in Suga's room with the other girls.

Jinx had decided that Wren was not so bad after all. She had seen another side of her—an entirely unexpected one. Yes, Wren, like everyone else, had her own problems. Wren had not handled them very well, but not everyone does. And Wren was trying to change for the better. Jinx would help her as much as she could. After all, they were sister Rhodesians.

Wallis returned to her alcove and her Japanese roommates and their highly effective room heater.

Wren, Freya, and Jinx returned to their thin mattresses and wool blankets next to the large fireplace in Suga's room. That night, the girls all roasted marshmallows in the fireplace. The sugary treats were the perfect antidote for the wintery conditions that had found their way into the Victorian residence hall.

Jinx was happy to be back at school because Muddy Hills meant being close to Rex. Jinx wondered how Rex had spent the weekend while she had been away. The flannel pyjama clad Jinx tapped on the screen of her smartphone while lying in bed near the fireplace. She was about to send Rex a text message, and then decided against it. No, it was late. Rex needed to sleep. Rex, like Jinx, not only had the play to prepare for but also exams. Jinx plugged her cell phone into its charger and then went to bed.

LONDON

Louise returned to her room that evening after having had sweet potatoes for dinner (again) in the vegan dining hall with Aurelia. Louise had asked for hot chocolate, only to discover that hot chocolate had been banned by the university because chocolate was product of brutal exploitation and environmental degradation.

After dinner, Aurelia was still hungry, so she ordered a thin crust Hawaiian pizza from her favorite Albanian pizzeria and went downstairs to the lobby of the residence hall to wait for the delivery driver—with hordes of other girls in the residence hall who were waiting for their dinners to be delivered after retreating from the bland vegan fare offered in the cafeteria.

Louise and Aurelia had spent most of the day studying in the library. The university's cavernous library was an architectural monstrosity. A large modern concrete structure of Brutalist design. It looked, as the Prince of Wales might say, as a place that incinerated, not harbored books.

Louise had discovered that many of the books had been withdrawn from circulation because they were now considered 'culturally insensitive'. Hundreds of books had vanished from the shelves overnight. And hundreds, perhaps thousands more, were soon to join them in the dustbin of literary history as soon as a student committee could decide which ones needed to go next. Decisions, decisions.

Louise had also heard rumors that soon even the Chemistry Department would be 'decolonized' by a special committee. Really. Louise didn't want to return to the second tier university in London in January. She wished that she could just transfer immediately to Midlands-Hasegawa with Aurelia. The 'safe spaces' at Louise's university in London were anything but. The university had become completely toxic to her and Aurelia.

The strawberry blonde Louise, in faded blue jeans, a white cotton blouse, and blue blazer, sat down at her modern white laminate desk. She turned on her laptop computer. She looked out the window as the computer sprang to life.

Outside the window was London; it was dark, and a light snow was falling. Louise loved snow; however, surrounded by the woke gloominess of her university, she could only sigh. Louise typed her password into the glowing screen. It was time to check her email.

Prometheus Occidental Publishing Ltd.

Dear Miss Percival,

Thank you for submitting your manuscript to Prometheus Occidental. We have read your novel and would like to publish it.

We find the story to be quite compelling. The editors were surprised to learn of your age, and that this is your first novel. We, at Prometheus Occidental, are confident that it will be able to find an audience.

We would like to meet with you in person at our offices in London as soon as possible. Please let us know when you are available.

Sincerely,

M.C. Sayers
Contract Manager
Occidental Prometheus Publishing

MIDLANDS-HASEGAWA UNIVERSITY
The large room on the first floor of the girls' residence hall was dark, save
for the orange glow of the room heater and the embers in the fireplace.
Suga and Pasha lay in their beds; Freya, Wren, and Jinx were asleep on thin
mattresses under wool blankets on the hardwood floor next to the large
marble fireplace. They were all dark shapes outlined in shadow.

Ping.

Freya stirred. Her smartphone was plugged into the charger next to her
mattress. The cell phone's screen had glowed momentarily with the
incoming message.

Ping.

Freya opened her eyes. The screen glowed and then faded. Freya, still laying
on her side under a wool blanket, unplugged the phone and looked at the
screen. She tapped on it and a text message appeared.

**My dear Freya, my novel has been accepted by a publisher in
London. My novel is going to be published. I can't believe it. I am so
happy.**

Freya smiled. She felt a sudden rush of adrenaline race through her. Freya
quickly tapped out a message.

Ping.

Freya read the message and smiled. She carefully and quietly got out of bed
and walked to the door of the room. She took her blue quilted jacket off of

a wooden peg on the wall and opened the door. It creaked a little as she carefully opened it. Light from the hallway lamps briefly flooded into the room. It disappeared as Freya carefully and quietly closed the door behind her.

THE HALLWAY

Freya, in a pair of blue and purple tartan pyjama bottoms (with a white draw string), a white t-shirt, white slippers, and wearing a blue quilted jacket, tapped on the screen. A moment later a voice answered.

'Freya! Isn't it wonderful?' said Louise excitedly.

'Yes. Louise, I knew that one day you would be a successful writer. I am really happy for you.'

'Thank you, Freya. I'm going to visit the editors at the London office tomorrow. Aurelia is going with me. I'm sorry for texting you so late.'

Freya could hear a voice in in the background. It sounded like Aurelia's.

'Aurelia said to say "hello",' said Louise happily.'

'Tell her I said "hello" too,' replied Freya quietly. She didn't want to wake anyone up. Freya held the smartphone up and looked at the time: 1:12am. Freya put the phone back up to her ear. She could hear someone chewing something.

'I'm eating cold pizza. Aurelia ordered one earlier. It's fantastic. I can't wait to transfer to Muddy Hills. Are there any pizza places up there?' asked Louise.

'Yes. There are two. They both serve excellent pizza. And the cafeteria here is almost as good as All Saints. They serve lasagna at least once a month.'

'Freya, do you think we could transfer to Muddy Hills in January? I know we missed the deadline, but does Muddy Hills ever make exceptions?'

'I don't know. Perhaps. I know my grandparents in Mayfair have a connection to the school. Maybe they could pull some strings?'

'Oh, if it is possible, we would be so happy. You have no idea how terrible things have become here in London. **The Winter Palace has fallen.** For sure.'

'I'm so sorry to hear that, Louise. Don't worry. Let me see what I can do. My grandparents love you. If they can get you into Muddy Hills, they will.'

'Thank you, Freya.'

Freya could hear the sound of the mini-refrigerator door closing over the phone.

'I'm going to send a copy of my book to my father. I doubt he will read it, but I am going to mail him a copy anyway.'

Freya understood. Louise desperately wanted her father to value her. To want her in his life. Poor little Louise was all alone in the world. Freya had been blessed with a kind and caring father. Freya could not understand Louise's father at all. Louise had shown Freya several photos of her late mother, and she was almost shocked by her appearance. Louise was a carbon copy of her late mother. Perhaps that was what had driven her father away from her? Louise's father could not stand to be reminded of his wife.

'I'm going to buy a dozen copies. I will add them to the libraries at the family pile and at my homes in London.'

'Oh, thank you, Freya. But I will give you a copy.'

'Please sign it for me, Louise.'

'I will', said Louise sleepily.

'Louise, we both need to get some sleep. Okay?'

'You're right. Good night, Freya. I'll see you in a week and half.'

Gemma—The Carthage Option—The Central Bank

SEOUL

It was snowing in Seoul that afternoon. The Asian megacity was blanketed in snow and ice. Millions of people went about their daily lives completely unaware of what was happening around them. The financial upheaval emanating from London had reached their shores and was quietly and stealthy wreaking havoc.

Only a few in the country had truly understood the enormity of the situation the country was facing.

THE BANK OF KOREA

The central banker, in coat and tie, pressed on the remote and another chart appeared on the screen.

'As you can see, the moves being made across the markets appear to be coordinated. This does not appear to be the actions of disparate groups or individuals. I believe this is the work of one group, or, perhaps, an individual,' said the senior central banker.

There was an audible gasp from those gathered in the conference room.

Across from the central banker was a long table that had been placed horizontally in front of the screen. Seated at the table were a dozen men and women. The audience, all high-ranking government officials, sat in the darkened room illuminated only by the large screen on the wall. These shadowy figures had remained silent while the central banker, a man tasked with protecting the country's financial reserves, gave his presentation.

It was too audacious to be true. Impossible. How was a lone group, or, even more unbelievably, an individual, able to carry out such an operation as this?

'Could this, perhaps, be the work of a foreign government?' asked the slender and attractive silver haired cabinet minister as she carefully studied the chart on the glowing screen.

'Yes, possibly,' replied the central banker. 'We have, thus far, been unable to find where this group or individual is operating from. But I am almost sure that all of this is the work of one group. I am inclined to believe that this is not the work of a foreign government.'

'Why not?' asked the minister.

'My next three slides will illustrate why,' said the central banker. He pointed the remote at the screen and a large map covered with arrows and crisscrossed with lines appeared.

A stunned silence followed.

Gemma—The Carthage Option—The Stone Cottage

THE LAKE DISTRICT
The stone cottage stood at the edge of a snowy field. It had been built more than a hundred years before and had once housed the family of a local farmer. Now this small cottage was the modest domicile of an English baron. Lord Mars Arthur Noel, the 13th Baron, had purchased the cottage a few months earlier. Its walls held what was left of the baron's worldly possessions.

The Honourables, Poppy and Violet, had driven out to see Mars in Poppy's silver Citroën. The little hatchback had been returned to her when Brian and Cordelia had driven up to the Lake District from London for the fox hunt at Violet's family pile in Northumberland. This was the first time Poppy had been behind the wheel of an automobile since the wedding last June. She was elated. The little car meant freedom. Today she had decided to accept Mars' invitation to tea at his home several miles away in Cumbria.

Poppy, in a pair of dark khaki wool trousers, a white cotton blouse, a blue quilted Burberry jacket, and a Burberry scarf, sat in a pre-war worn leather arm chair. Violet, clad in country tweeds, sat on a sofa that was the same pale color of blue as Violet's eyes. Violet, her long glossy blonde hair resting on dark blue, tangerine, and light grey tartan shoulders of her tweed jacket, smiled. She was happy to be sitting in Mars' stone cottage with Poppy. A few weeks ago, she had almost lost Poppy, and now they were about to be served tea on a wintery afternoon.

Yes, the small main room of the house had a definite aristocratic air about it. The white walls were adorned with several silver and leather framed photos, many of them black and white and quite old, of the 13th Baron's illustrious ancestors. There was a large gilt framed oil painting of the young 7th Baron which had been painted in the 1790s. The 7th Baron wore the embroidered blue coat of an English naval officer. The young baron had been killed at the Battle of the Nile. There were two smaller oil paintings, both with gilt frames, of the baron's former family pile (now owned by a foreign billionaire).

The hardwood floors had been restored before Mars moved in. It was partially covered by a gorgeous Persian rug that Mars had removed from the family's country house before it was sold to help pay off his late older brother's debts.

The highly polished coffee table was new. The pale blue (wool) sofa and the two heavily worn whisky brown leather armchairs were not. They had been rescued from the country house in Sussex before the sale.

Near the door to one of the (two) bedrooms, was a slender wooden bookshelf filled with books.

There was another, much larger bookshelf, on the opposite white wall. On one shelf there was a cricket bat that Mars had purchased while at Eton. A silver framed photo of the Eton cricket team resplendent in cricket whites, had been placed next to the wooden bat. A very young James and Mars stood next to each other in the group photo. The rest of the shelves were filled with books—some of them over two hundred years old.

There was something about the effortless luxury of the decor; the aristocratic insouciance, the classic style and placement of the paintings, books, and furniture, that came naturally to an English Hon like Mars. Mars was one of them. Yes, all three of them, Poppy, Violet, and Mars, were imbued with the true spirit of the Hon.

THE HONS

Being a Hon was more than just style and manner. It was a question of patriotism, the awareness of what it meant to be English, noble, and the love—yes—the love of country, tradition, and the English people.

True Hons were disappearing from the English landscape. Tradition no longer mattered in England. The very traditional values of the country that had made an absolute monarchy into a constitutional one and had turned little England into a vast global empire were no longer wanted. Reforms of the House of Lords in 1999 had seen most of the hereditary nobility expelled and replaced by Life Peers of sometimes dubious natures. The English nobility had already been largely replaced by high flying moneyed celebrities—who were often vulgar and badly educated, if educated at all. The *neo-ploutos* were usually unpatriotic, openly despised the English flag of St George, and often openly championed foreign countries, peoples, and causes. Were these people the future leaders of England? If so, how would England survive?

It wouldn't.

Unless the current trajectory could be changed—by someone.

But who?

THE MAIN ROOM

'A hot cup of tea is *rather* nice on a cold winter's day such as this,' said Mars as he entered the main room carrying a silver tray, a sterling silver tea pot, and three white bone china tea cups and saucers. There was also a glass jar with a sterling silver lid with sugar cubes, three silver spoons, and a glass jar of honey. Mars placed the tray on the highly polished coffee table.

Mars, in a pair of dark khaki trousers and a white dress shirt, served tea. Mars' brown hair seemed to have grown greyer overnight. Perhaps it was the recent events with Poppy? Or perhaps, like everyone else, the 47-year-old Mars was just getting older.

Poppy held the tea cup in her soft manicured hands for a moment and inhaled the steam which rose from it. 'This is quite nice, Mars. Thank you.'

'I bought this tea from a small tea shop in the local village,' said Mars. 'I have some biscuits in the kitchen. I'll think you'll like them.'

'Yes, the tea is *marvellous*,' said Violet in her posh and Sloaney intonation.

Mars smiled. 'I'll be right back. The biscuits come from a bakery in Primrose Hill.' Mars then nodded slightly and disappeared into his kitchen.

Violet looked out the one of the white sash windows of the cottage. Outside were snow clad fields, dry stone walls, and the occasional tree. The scenery was quite beautiful. The glow from the stone fireplace drew her attention from the view outside. The stone fireplace was filled with burning logs surrounded by bright orange glowing embers. Warmth and light radiated from the Edwardian stone surround. On the mantle was a small sterling silver box and a set of field glasses in a worn leather case with a long leather strap that had belonged to one of the 13th Baron's ancestors. They had been used in 1915 to call in artillery barrages on the Ottomans in the Dardanelles. The *bins* still functioned perfectly.

Poppy placed the tea cup on the saucer and leaned back into the soft armchair. She momentarily closed her eyes. Yes, she was tired. This short excursion had been surprisingly taxing.

Violet noticed Poppy (apparently) dozing off. Yes, Violet was a little worried. Soon, decided Violet, she would drive Poppy home.

'Yes, I brought the biscuits with me on train from London last night. Light short bread biscuits with custard buttercream fillings,' said Mars as he reappeared with a silver tray and a white bone chine plate of biscuits. He set them down quietly on the coffee table after noticing that Poppy had nodded off to sleep in the leather armchair.

Mars sat down in an armchair opposite the girls. Mars quietly poured himself a cup of the honey scented tea.

Poppy suddenly woke up.

'Would you like a buttercream custard biscuit, Poppy?' asked Mars.

'Yes. Thank you, Mars,' replied Poppy happily.

Mars then offered one to Violet. She took one. Mars was surprised. He hadn't seen Violet ever have any kind of biscuit, cake, or pastry.

Mars sipped his tea. The tea was fantastic.

Here, in a small stone cottage in the Lake District, far away from blighted London, they were warm and safe.

'These are heavenly,' said Violet as she nibbled at the small biscuit.

'Yes, you will have to give me the address of the bakery for when I return to London,' said Poppy.

'I will email you the address,' said Mars happily.

'Thank you, Mars. How long will you be staying in Cumbria?' asked Poppy.

'I will return to London tomorrow morning. I will return for the Christmas holidays on the 23rd. I won't have to return to London until the 3rd. It will be a nice break,' replied Mars.

'Mummy is looking forward to having you spend Christmas with us this year,' said Poppy and she smiled.

'Yes, it will be especially nice with all of the children this year. Oh, I have an extra box of biscuits for everyone at the house. I'm sure Henry and Lucy will like them,' said Mars.

'That's very nice of you. I'm sure every will appreciate it,' replied Poppy.

'Will Freya be spending Christmas in London or Northumberland this year?' asked Mars.

'Christmas Day in Northumberland and then she will take the train with Louise to London to spend time with her grandparents in Mayfair.'

'I really like Louise. She is really good hearted and intelligent,' said Mars.

'Yes, she's a real poppet,' said Violet happily. 'The girls would be lost with each other. They are practically sisters now.'

'When will you return to London, Poppy?' asked Mars.

'As soon as I can. I really miss London. I love being with the family here in the Lake District, but I do miss London. I want to get back to work. I miss the bank and the City. I miss Hungarian cuisine,' said Poppy, and she smiled.

Gemma—The Carthage Option—The Helix

LONDON
The City, that December, appeared calm. It was just a façade. In reality, the financial world was in a tailspin. Every effort was being made to conceal it. Repairing the damage; finding out what was actually transpiring, and who was behind it all, was secondary. Panicked clients would withdraw all of their money if they knew something was amiss. And everyone knew it.

MILLENNIUM INVESTMENTS
Gemma, in a navy blue pencil skirt, a white blouse, and wearing a pair of tortoise shell glasses, signed for the package at the front desk. The slender cardboard box was covered in airmail stickers and a clear plastic pouch that contained mailing addresses and a customs declaration. The package, from Singapore, had been sent by the branch office. Alexa had been expecting it.

163

Gemma tilted her reading glasses back on her head of glossy brown hair and carried the slender box into the main office. She walked over to Alexa's office and knocked lightly on the wooden door.

'Come in.'

'Here is the package from Singapore that you've been expecting,' said Gemma. Gemma then placed the box on Alexa's desk.

'Thank you, Gemma. Please have a seat. I would like to go over next week's schedule with you.'

Gemma sat down in the modern leather chair in front of Alexa's large and ultra modern desk. Behind Alexa, Gemma had a panoramic view of London. Gemma looked at her Cartier watch: 11:33am. London, on this wintery day, was shrouded in grey skies and falling snow. The view of London from the 12th floor (or was that the 10th floor?) was spectacular. Only this helix like structure offered views of the city like this; a view like nothing else in the world.

'What?' said Alexa to herself quietly as she began reading through the report.

Gemma turned her attention from the snowy scenery and looked at Alexa. She had gone pale. Gemma watched in silence as Alexa read through several pages of the report.

After a few minutes, Alexa looked up at her and said, 'Gemma, could you tell Tarquin and Allegra that I need to see them in my office?'

Gemma—The Carthage Option—The Private Bank

LONDON
Brian, in a dark grey suit, pale blue dress shirt, and a dark blue tartan necktie, studied the report carefully. He read through page after page of analysis, graphs, and charts. The most important financial reports were never emailed or stored online at the bank. Only paper documents and

reports were compiled. Senior members of the staff typed up the reports themselves and few copies of them were ever made. Important financial documents were kept in the bank's large vault under guard. That was a long-held policy. Now, because of the current situation, it had been expanded to include a wider variety of lesser materials. **Yes, the Internet was a double-edged sword.** One could learn a lot from it, but the Internet could also be used to spy on those who used it. The Internet allowed access, but that access went both ways. Once that door had been opened, it could not easily be closed.

Brian had been navigating the current financial maelstrom extraordinarily well. He had been promoted to vice president of the bank the day before. The retiring vice president had had enough. He had found himself a worn at old man at fifty-four. The former vice president knew that what the bank and the entire financial world was facing was calamitous. There would be no escape from what was coming. Yes, it was better to retire and retreat to the countryside. Brian Atherton, easily the most insightful, hardworking, and financially savvy member of the staff, was the obvious choice to replace him. Brian had accepted the position, not out of personal ambition, but out of a sense of loyalty to the bank and its clients. Now was not the time to abandon ship.

Brian found the entire situation to be deeply troubling. The most troubling aspects of the situation were that the identity of the people behind the upheaval and their true motivations had remained a mystery. And, to make matters worse, they attacked unseen and had, so far, proven impossible to trace. These pirates (or pirate) understood how to use technology in ways few, if any, could. The bank's technical team had failed to locate any trace of them. How was that possible? Were these financial raids being carried out by a foreign government?

Brian had little doubt that, if the bank survived, he would become its next president. That would mean a lot more responsibility. It would also be a well-earned reward for decades of hard work and loyalty. But the bank would have to survive the financial storm it now found itself in. His predecessor, an intelligent man and experienced banker that Brian respected, had felt the situation was hopeless. Was it?

In spite of everything that staff at the bank had been able to fend off, the bank was slowly being bled white.

Brian completed the report and then placed it on the desk in front of him. He leaned back in the leather chair and looked out the window. It was snowing. The London that appeared before him was of dark shapes, grey skies, and white snow. In the distance, Brian could see the crystalline Shard. The towering spire of glass, the tallest structure in London, stood out against the overcast sky. The Shard was a titanic multisided mirror. The falling white snow and the grey of the skies were reflected in it. Brian wondered if the people behind the approaching financial catastrophe now wandered its glassy halls. Brian wondered if the people working in its offices truly understood the enormity of what was about to befall all of them.

Brian looked at the glowing screen of his smartphone. The train to the Lake district would depart in three hours. Behind Brian's desk was a leather box suitcase. Brian would go directly to the train station after work. He wanted to see Poppy and his children. Brian had learned a lesson: never take those you love for granted. Brian always felt his heart tighten when he thought about what had happened to Poppy. He had almost lost her. Almost. God had given him a second chance, and, unlike many, he would not squander it.

5 ANOTHER COUNTRY

Gemma—The Carthage Option—The Dragon

ANOTHER COUNTRY

It was mid-December, and the entire country was blanketed in a deep layer of snow. Eastern Europe was a very cold place in the winter—this winter had been proving to be exceptionally brutal.

Three men had just climbed out of a white UAZ-469. The vehicle had been purchased by one of Carter Holland's agents in The Czech Republic (now officially known as Czechia, formally part of the Austro-Hungarian Empire, part of which had once been known as the kingdom of Bohemia). Carter Holland had purchased over three hundred of them. They would be used by his new army. Any suspicion at the appearance of a fleet of new UAZs would be misdirected towards the semi-literate thugs now occupying the Kremlin. A good, if most likely momentary, distraction.

The Revenant, in a pair of khaki wool trousers, brown leather Chelsea boots, a dark blue hooded duffle coat, and wool gloves, led the small group of foreign mercenaries. They walked through the forest of beech trees; icy winds swirled around them. The sky above was a series of grey and white clouds that churned and eddied in the harsh northern winds. In the distance were huge and majestic snow-capped mountains. And not a soul could be seen with the exception of the three men trudging through the deep snow.

The second man, a Texan, breathed hard against the icy cold air. The Texan was wearing a dark blue winter parka, faded blue jeans, and leather cowboy boots. At the Revenant's request, he had left his weathered cowboy hat back home in Terrell. The Revenant didn't want the Texan drawing too much attention to himself as wondered around the dilapidated city at the edge of the world. The man did, however, wear one of his highly engraved sterling silver rodeo belt buckles.

The third man, a former British para, wore a knee length dark grey wool overcoat with a light-colored fur collar and a pair of faded blue jeans. The Englishman had flipped the collar up to help protect his head from the icy winds.

All three mercenaries carried pistols. The Revenant had insisted on being armed. One of Carter Holland's local operatives had supplied them with them at the hotel an hour after they had arrived on a domestic airline flight.

The small turbo prop plane had landed at the large and largely disused airport that afternoon. The rundown airport terminal was a surviving remnant of ugly 1970s Soviet style décor. The slovenly and unprofessional airport staff had been rude and unhelpful. One of Carter Holland's local agents had met them in the nearly empty terminal. The local operative was in his mid-twenties, clean cut, physically fit, intelligent, and unexpectantly polite. The local operative spoke English flawlessly. But, then again, Carter Holland paid well and expected efficiency, even in a place like this.

After ordering and tasting the inedible meal offered at the hotel restaurant and being served by the decidedly lazy and unfriendly staff, the local agent was telephoned and he delivered several cans of American and Japanese canned foods and bottled water from France an hour later. The three mercenaries had dinner together in one of the hotel rooms. Outside, the snow fell and the winds howled. The rooms, however, were warm. The men got a good night's sleep.

The forlorn, polluted, and broken city at the end of the world had shocked the former British para and the Texan. The Revenant had seen worse. This hollowed out shell was to be Carter Holland's capital? Impossible thought the Englishman. The pot holed streets and largely abandoned city was filled with communist bloc eyesores and the occasional dead tree. As the men drove through the city, they were surprised by how few people appeared on the streets. How many people lived here?

The harbor, with its rusting cranes and collapsing warehouses was virtually unusable. It was, however, usable enough for the project. Yes, the project, a multi-billion dollar effort that would easily succeed. The Revenant could feel in his bones that it would all come together. The half-sunk Soviet built submarine (which had been supplied to its former Warsaw Pact ally) in the harbor only added to the place's post-apocalyptic feel.

The road out of the city was smooth. Carter had paid to have the roads repaved (properly). The men drove out of the city in silence. After two hours of driving through deserted or nearly deserted villages and past abandoned farm land, the white UAZ entered a thick forest choked with snow. The roads were snow covered and it was difficult to navigate them sometimes. Eventually the vehicle made it to the clearing marked in red ink and yellow highlighter on the folded paper tactical map.

THE RIVER
Jem, the former British para from Surrey, stood in the center of the clearing in the forest and stared at the jagged and gigantic mountains which ringed the forest.

'You know, even by the abysmally low standards of Eastern Europe, that city is a Shite hole,' said Jem.

The Texan smiled and looked at the Revenant. 'Jem's never been one for tact, has he?'

'No. But I appreciate his candor. Sometimes,' replied the Revenant.

The Revenant pointed to the wide river ahead of them. It stretched for miles in either direction. It banks were covered in snow and it was partially frozen over with a thin layer of ice. Along both sides of the river were barren beech trees that swayed in the cold wind.

'Here. This river will be the natural border of the new country. A fake regional independence movement will apparently break out in the city and the surrounding region. We will quickly kill the local policemen and militia units, and then, the rebels—that's us—will seize the city's only functioning radio station and declare independence. A new country will have been born. Carter Holland has bribed all the necessary people in the government and military. This country breathes corruption. The country's President, Ministers of Security, Defense, Transportation, and Energy are all on the payroll, as well as half a dozen key generals. The upcoming civil war will be an opportunity for the President to declare martial law, kill his rivals, and purge the officer corps of potential troublemakers—probably by sending them to be killed fighting against us. Then the President can consolidate his power and rule forever. And the President and the rest of the traitors surrounding him will become fantastically wealthy. The President will then concede defeat, recognize the independence of the breakaway country, and Carter Holland will have his own country. No one in this rundown nation cares about this part of the country, not really. This region has been abandoned for decades. No one from here will quit their low paying restaurant jobs in London or give up working as a day laborer on construction sites in Berlin to fly home to defend this place,' said the Revenant.

'I can't believe that Carter Holland has chosen this piece of dirt to build a new country. The people here are some of the worst I've ever met in my life. And most of them appear to be over sixty, alcoholic, and near death. Where are most of the young? Probably trafficked. Who will populate this new country?' asked Jem.

'I don't know. Colonists, I suppose,' said the Revenant, his breath materializing around him in the wintery air. The Revenant looked at the mountainous, snow-capped terrain before him. The mountain peaks were partially shrouded in dark clouds. The contrast between the white snow and the dark grey clouds was stark and otherworldly. Here, at the end of the world, everything took on a ghostly and almost supernatural air.

This was a beautiful country filled with ugly cities and even uglier people.

The Revenant pivoted to look at the other mercenaries. 'Thousands, probably tens of thousands, of the natives will be kept around to maintain some semblance of legitimacy—for a while. Most of the local population is now elderly and lives in poverty. Holland will buy them off. There is no true patriotism left here. This entire region has been depopulated. The central government abandoned these people in early 1990s. The younger people that are still here are usually either alcoholic or drug addled. Or both. Holland has already had a political manifesto prepared in a dozen languages. The propaganda team Holland has put together is working overtime. He has thought of everything. The uprising will appear to those both within and outside of the country as a legitimate separatist movement with legitimate grievances. Local quislings will act as the puppet government until Carter Holland decides to take power officially for himself. I've arranged to arm and equip a local militia with surplus uniforms, leather and canvas webbing and kit, and boots from old Warsaw Pact warehouses. I'm only going to supply them with surplus SKS and Mosin-Nagant rifles, bayonets, and a dozen bullets each. A few thousand surplus gas masks will also be handed out. Just enough to make it look like there is a rebel army made up of locals. But not well armed enough to cause us any trouble. The core army and the combat drones will do all of the real fighting,' said the Revenant.

'Do you really think this will work?' asked the parka-clad Texan as he stood between too tall birch trees, crossed his arms, and rubbed his shoulders, trying to stay warm.

'Yes. It will work. Everything is in order at this end. Now, it all depends on what happens at Carter Holland's end in London. It will be Carter Holland that the success of this operation will depend,' replied the Revenant.

The slender and athletic Texan nodded. If the Revenant believed that the uprising would work, then it would. The Texan was confident of that.

'And what if Carter Holland's end fails?' asked Jem in a West Country dialect. 'What will we do then, mate?'

'He won't fail. However, let's say he does. I have an escape plan for the core soldiers. Not all of us will be able to make it out. No, that is unlikely. But, that is part of the risk we all take. That is why you are all to be paid in advanced—in full. I will see to that before we move,' said the Revenant. 'I will be one of the last to leave the city, if things fall apart. I will be one of the last to leave the theater of operations. I will get as many of the men out as possible,' said the Revenant.

'Could I have a look at those escape plans before we move?' asked Jem.

'Yes. Of course. If you like. I will show them to you when we return to London. But let's not get ahead of ourselves. I am confident this operation will succeed,' replied the Revenant. The Revenant started to turn towards the river as he spoke. 'Carter Holland understands many things that most do not. He knows what he is doing. **And I know what I am doing**,' said the Revenant in his indeterminable foreign accent.

The Revenant then started to walk towards the rivers' edge, the snow crunching underfoot. The other two men did not follow him. The sky grew slightly darker as the Revenant approached the wide river. He walked to the river's edge and stopped.

The Revenant looked skyward: the grey and white clouds grew murkier as he gazed at them. The gigantic granite mountains took on a phantasmagoric appearance. The jagged mountain peaks seem to shift and change amongst the clouds. The grey and white clouds eddied and churned above him. A cold gust of wind suddenly rose up from the frozen black waters of the river and chilled the Revenant to the bone. He looked down into its rushing waters. The water was dark, black, and pieces of ice floated down the waterway. The ice flows were everywhere; pieces of ice floated quickly down the dark river.

Suddenly, seemingly thousands of pieces of ice seemed to rise to the surface of the water and formed into intricate patterns and ornate shapes. The ice churned and, as if put quickly into order by some supernatural hand, took shape. The ice flows moving down the river now resembled the scintillating scales of a dragon. The entire river was a dragon. There was the body. And along the river banks, the wings. And there, just below the Revenant, and staring up at him with inky black eyes, was the head of the dragon. The Revenant shuddered—out of fear. The icy head of the dragon turned slowly to look directly into the Revenant's eyes. The Revenant was rooted to the frozen snow-covered ground. The Revenant's eyes widened. All the color drained out of the Revenant's face. The Revenant could feel the icy cold breath of the black dragon as its head rose from the dark waves. The Revenant tried to look away, but he couldn't. He was transfixed. He tried to cry out, but he couldn't. Tears formed in the Revenant's eyes as the dragon's gaze intensified. Once more he felt the icy breath of the black dragon on his face. Once more he failed to turn away. The dragon slowly lowered its head back into the black waters of the churning river. Slowly, very slowly, the dragon's body broke apart and flowed down the river. The last part of the dragon to disappear into the water was the dragon's head, which the Revenant could swear had **smiled at him** before it fell to icy pieces and vanished into the waters of the black river.

The Revenant stood and stared into the swirling waters of the icy river. The Revenant's stare was vacant, as if he was in a trance.

'Hey…Hey! Are you alright?' asked the Texan as he trudged through the deep snow towards the Revenant. 'I've been shouting at you for the last five minutes. Jem's got the heater going in the car. Let's drive back to the city and get something to eat. We'll freeze to death if we stay out here much longer.'

'What?' asked the Revenant quietly.

'Let's get back to the city, okay?' replied the Texan.

The Revenant snapped out of the trance and turned around to face the Texan. 'Did you see that?'

'See what?' asked the Texan through chattering teeth.

The Revenant turned around and looked into the icy waters of the river. Nothing. The Revenant turned back around and looked at the Texan.

'Let's go,' said the Revenant.

Gemma—The Carthage Option—The Quislings

ANOTHER COUNTRY

The army general stood 5'11". He was corpulent and ugly; the first thing one noticed about him was his huge double chin. It made him look like a bullfrog. He had a large belly, but his legs were skinny and bow-legged. He had a big head, beady eyes, and naturally curly brown hair that appeared to be the result of a cheap salon treatment. The sides of his head were shaved, when he took off his army cap, a shock of curly brown hair burst forth. It was unmilitary, unprofessional, thought the foreign soldiers present at the meeting. This was what a local army general looked like here?

This was the man that would officially lead the rebel army. He was a remnant of the former communist army. He had graduated from a military academy and had served in a variety of different army units. The general's uniform was heavily beribboned, as seem to be normal in Eastern Europe; the number of ribbons a soldier wore seemed to increase the farther east one went. It had appeared that the Bullfrog had been awarded one ribbon for every day of service.

The Bullfrog was a heavy drinker and a heavy smoker. He was married, but the marriage was a miserable one. The Bullfrog spent whatever money he had on vice. The general looked like walking hepatitis.

The Bullfrog, surprisingly, wasn't very bright. He thought of himself as a genius, which is something that most stupid people who attain any kind of position at all usually think. The Bullfrog had attained his sole star through attrition and office politics. He had a friend, a civil servant in the defense ministry, a long-time friend from the same village that the Bullfrog had been born in, who made sure that the Bullfrog was eventually promoted. The commands he had always been given, were, not surprisingly, the ones no one else wanted.

The Bullfrog had been given the command of this region because it was godforsaken and miserable. It was boring here. There was little in the way of nightlife. The troops he commanded were the dregs of the army. They were the slovenly recruits who had joined the military out of desperation. Many of them had criminal records. They were ill-disciplined, unemployable, and physically and mentally unfit for military service. They were pathetic creatures. The soldiers wore mismatched used uniforms which sometimes still bore the old communist insignia almost thirty years after the collapse of European communism. Thousands of these soldiers were garrisoned here at the end of the world.

The Bullfrog would lead them all into a trap. They would be the first to die. And no one would care.

The Bullfrog had been promised millions of dollars, a half dozen expensive cars, and the command of the future imperial army. In reality, he would command a few thousand lightly armed militia. They would do little, if any fighting. They would simply patrol the streets and be filmed by Carter Holland's propaganda teams. A few decent, presentable, well kitted out, native quislings would speak to the international press. Carter Holland had decided that the Bullfrog would not be one of the them. He was a shambling mound, an embarrassment. The Bullfrog was just another tool in the tool box of revolution. When the new country's independence was secured, the Bullfrog would be 'assassinated' by agents from the capital. The duplicitous President would claim vengeance. A national traitor would have been killed at the instigation of the heroic President. But the men who would kill the Bullfrog would not come from the capital, they would be the men now sitting in the back room of a rickety and decaying tea house.

'Yes. I will order a column of soldiers to take over the old cement factory. I will send almost all of my soldiers there. They will travel in a column of trucks and armored vehicles—back-to-back,' said the Bullfrog laughingly. 'And when the column turns onto the approach to the factory, your soldiers will ambush them. Don't worry. My officers are incompetent. Half the soldiers will be drunk. You have no idea how worthless these soldiers really are. The defense ministry does. That's why they sent them here. You should be able to kill them all within twenty or thirty minutes. I will send the remainder of my soldiers to help them. You will dispose of them all quickly. Of course, most of the soldiers will run away when the shooting starts. It will be like hunting mice,' said the fat Bullfrog in his heavily accented English.

'How will you slip away unnoticed?' asked the Texan.

'Simple, I will just turn left at the intersection instead of right. I will escape in the confusion. I will meet you and the others at the hotel, as planned,' said the Bullfrog.

'General,' said the Revenant, 'The militia will be assembled in three different places in the city. They will requisition the remaining armored vehicles and heavy tanks and head to their preplanned positions. My soldiers in the core army will do all the fighting. All you have to do is command the militia. Do you understand?' asked the Revenant.

'Yes. No problem. I know what to do,' said the Bullfrog as he checked the time on his expensive Swiss wristwatch (a gift from Carter Holland).

'Why are you wearing that watch?' asked the Revenant. 'Don't you realize that it will draw attention to you?' asked the Revenant in mildly accented English.

'Every army general in this country wears a Swiss wristwatch. All of us do. No one will say anything about it,' snarled the Bullfrog indignantly.

Jem, seated in the corner of the room with a window on either side of him, clinched his fists. He wanted to beat this fat, beady eyed creature to death right there. Jem had taken an instant dislike to the native population of the country. The natives were rude, vulgar, and dishonest. The last three days in the country had only solidified that dislike. Jem had seen the very soldiers the general commanded shaking the locals down at check points throughout the city. Some of the soldiers were drunk at their posts. But here, in this dilapidated backroom of a rundown tea shop, Jem found himself feeling sorry for them. Jem never thought he would, but the Bullfrog was selling out his own men. He was conniving with foreigners to send his own soldiers to their deaths. To Jem, **the Bullfrog was just another bad officer.** Jem had met a lot of them. The Bullfrog was typical of them.

THE TEA HOUSE

The tea house had never been a nice establishment. It was built for factory workers and their families in the 1960s. It was state run until 1992, when the manager simply walked out the door one night and never returned. He hadn't even bothered to lock the doors or turn off the lights. Communism had failed and he was now jobless. A local pensioner, a retired violinist with a state orchestra, had taken it over and now served cups of inexpensive tea that came in small red boxes from India. The tea wasn't bad.

The main room had a dozen wooden tables and several cheap gold (painted) framed photos of Lenin and communist generals in gaudy uniforms.

The backroom was reserved for private meetings. The old woman who ran the tea house never asked any questions. She just pocketed a few Euros or US dollars from the men when they reserved the room. She would leave an old cheap kettle, a few chipped tea cups, a plastic bag of sugar, and a red box of Indian tea on the corner table next to a small stove for the expected visitors. The room was entered through a side door that opened into an alleyway. People could enter and leave this neutral ground unseen. It was here, in this back room covered in peeling garish 1970s wallpaper, that a group of people was meeting to determine that fate of the people of the entire region.

The tea house was also ideal for clandestine meetings because the neighborhood was practically abandoned. Only a few dozen elderly lived in the surrounding crumbling apartment blocks. Most of the units in the buildings had been abandoned in the early 1990s. At night, one could count the number of illuminated windows in each apartment building on one hand.

The only other business that operated on the pot holed street was a small makeshift corner store that sold low-quality canned goods. Cigarettes and alcohol were only available at a few stores in the city controlled by a local gangster. The owner of the corner store was a haggard and bent old woman in her early 70s. She was a retired rocket scientist and had once worked on engine projects. Now, alone in the world, she lived in a rundown flat with no hot water and only occasional electricity. Her husband drank himself to death in the 90s; her children had immigrated to Canada and forgotten her. Now, she survived on a pension that couldn't even cover the cost of her medication and the merger earnings she made from the store. She had grown up without God in a godless country; but now, in this place, she wished she could find Him. Perhaps it would grant her some peace? She had tried to find God in her nightly prayers, but He apparently had had no interest in her. Or perhaps He did? How would this old woman have felt if she knew that her fate now lay in the hands of a foreigner far away in London?

The Bullfrog had arrived in an olive drab UAZ jeep he had driven himself. He had parked it behind the building and entered through the side door unseen in the darkness. Not that it really mattered. No one living in this area would have cared. Nothing ever happened in this city. The residents now simply waited for their empty lives to end.

The Revenant looked out one of the windows and noticed that it had started to snow again. He looked down at the paper map spread out on the table. It had been heavily marked with red, blue, and black ink and a yellow highlighter. The Texan, in faded blue jeans, a white button-down Oxford dress shirt, and a pair of brown leather cowboy boots, studied the map carefully. Jem, studied the Bullfrog as the general took shot after shot of vodka from a bottle that he had brought with him to the meeting.

'What about the local naval units? How will they react when the shooting starts?' asked the Texan.

Before the Revenant could answer, the Bullfrog, festooned like a Christmas tree in cheap tin and enameled medals, and three sheets to the wind, shouted, 'There are no naval units here!' The red faced general then slumped back into the wooden chair.

The Revenant cast a disdainful glance towards the inebriated general and said, 'The navy withdrew in the early 1990s. The naval facilities have all but rotted to pieces.'

'How long before we can expect a reaction from the capital?' asked the Texan.

'The President has agreed to delay sending in reinforcements for at least three days,' replied the Revenant quietly. 'The President will send in units of commanded by politically unreliable officers. The general in charge of the reinforcements is on the payroll. He will botch the operation. The president wants the officers in these units killed. They are dangerous political rivals. After most of them are dead, he will move against his remaining rivals in the capital. After a few months of phony war, the region will be allowed to breakaway. It seems incredible, I know, but this is how many of these countries in Eastern and Southeastern Europe operate now. There are no governments left here; there are only the facades of governments,' said the Revenant. 'Most of these countries are just a collection of mafia fiefdoms. Nothing more.'

The blurry-eyed Bullfrog swayed back and forth in the worn wooden chair. The general's large epaulettes glittered in stark contrast to the bloated dark red face that rested at a lopsided angle between them. The Bullfrog suddenly slumped forward onto the table; it was only the agility of the Texan that the tactical map was pulled away before the general could plant his fat, drooling face in it. The Bullfrog had blacked out.

The meeting was adjourned.

The three foreign mercenaries put on their coats, gathered their things, and left the backroom through the side entrance. They left the Bullfrog face down on the table.

When Jem opened the side door, a blast of freezing cold air entered the room. The three men filed out and shut the door behind them. They walked to the white UAZ jeep and climbed in. The Revenant started the engine, turned on the headlights, and drove slowly down the alleyway. When he reached the main street, he looked both ways, and then turned slowly out onto the wide boulevard. It was snowing lightly.

The Revenant drove; the Texan sat in the front passenger seat; Jem sat in the back of the UAZ. The vehicle moved slowly down the darkened street. None of the street lamps worked in this part of the city.

'When the operation is over, and the new country secure, can I kill the general?' asked Jem.

The Revenant looked into the rearview mirror at Jem's handsome, if middle aged face. Jem, buttoned up in his dark grey wool overcoat, its fur collar flipped up and partially framing his face, stared back at him with a blank, tired gaze.

'Sure.'

Gemma—The Carthage Option—Under the Sheltering Sky

ANOTHER COUNTRY
The white UAZ jeep had stopped at the edge of the forest. Beyond was a snowy field, and beyond the field were the gigantic and snow-capped mountains. It was an overcast and grey day. It was snowing and a cold wind—cutting and merciless—bit into the three men who stood next to the white vehicle.

'They're late,' said the Texan, a lone figure clad in a navy blue parka, faded blue jeans, and black leather gloves. He had pulled the hood of his parka up over his head and only his cleanshaven, chiseled face could be seen.

'That seems to be part of the culture here,' said the Revenant; his breath could be seen materializing in the cold air around him.

Jem, the tall, slender, and powerfully built ex-Para looked at the mountain range that loomed up before him through a set of powerful binoculars. The field glasses had digital components that allowed for range finding and night vision with the push of a button.

Ping.

The Revenant looked at his encrypted smartphone. He read the text message and then tapped out a response on the screen and sent it.

'They want to meet us at a village seven miles north of here. I know where it is. I have it marked on my map,' said the Revenant.

The three mercenaries climbed into the Russian UAZ and drove off.

THE VILLAGE

The village had been abandoned for over two decades, and it looked like it. Three dozen small ramshackle structures clustered around a large central municipal building which was surrounded by large farm fields covered in a thick ocean of white snow. Abandoned Soviet era cars, light trucks, and tractors littered the village. It was as if everyone had just stopped what they were doing and simply walked away. Here and there large, leafless maple and beech trees stood in front of houses and lined the dirt roads of the former communist utopia.

The Revenant shifted and the white vehicle moved forward. Ahead, next to the central building, several brand new 469-UAZs and around dozen people could be seen. The white UAZ slowed as it entered the village.

Three white UAZ jeeps were parked along the edge of the street—at least what was once a street. The central building was surrounded by a dozen leafless European beech trees. The white washed building still bore a large plastic red star over the double door entrance. The weathered wooden doors were closed against the winter chill. Smoke could be seen rising from all three of the stone building's chimneys. The municipal building had been requisitioned by the revolution.

The Revenant parked in front of the central building. On the other side of the building was a dark blue 2018 Range Rover.

A slender middle-aged man with grey and white hair approached them. Clad in camouflage BDU trousers, black leather combat boots, a white camouflage waist length jacket that was unbuttoned and revealed a black mock turtle neck jumper. The man smiled. Jem was the first out of the vehicle.

'Bash! It's good to see you, mate!' said Jem happily.

The South African smiled.

'It's been a long time, Jem. You look the same, only older,' replied Bash with a smile. The South African kept his hair like a British army officer's. Bash was attractive. A former Atlas Cheetah jet fighter pilot who had flown hundreds of combat sorties against Cuban and Angolan Migs during the 80s and early 90s (and scored several aerial victories in the process), Bash had left his homeland and turned his talents to foreign endeavors, most, but not all, of which had paid exceedingly well.

'I see we are all here now,' said Bash. The svelte Bash was only about 5' 7". Jem towered over him. 'There is heat inside and decent food,' said Bash.

The Revenant and the Texan walked around the white SUV and shook hands with Bash. Yes, it was Bash. A long time comrade and a good and loyal friend.

'When is the demonstration scheduled?' asked the Revenant.

'It starts when you're ready, mate,' replied Bash.

THE CENTRAL BUILDING
The interior of the building looked to be exactly what it was: a former communist municipal building. The building had always been a crude utilitarian structure; decades of neglect had also taken a toll. The building had been hastily repaired by a crew of workers brought in by Carter Holland from London. They had had no contact with the locals and had worked in secret. The roof had been repaired along with the walls and

windows. The building had been replumbed and rewired. The interior had been repainted white. The large Soviet built emergency generator had also been repaired. The work completed, the construction crew returned to England.

Two of the Revenant's men, both English, stood in the lobby of the building. The mercenaries wore camouflage BDUs under a set of white camouflage and black leather combat boots. They wore holstered pistols and carried machine guns. They also wore body armor. Both former Paras were in their late 20s and nodded in acknowledgement when their commander entered the building.

'Good afternoon, sir,' said the taller of the two. The former Paras' radio chirped as he spoke.

'Good afternoon. Settled in?'

'Yes. But we are scheduled to depart tomorrow morning. It will be good to back in England after camping out here for the last three weeks,' said the former Para, and he smiled.

THE CONTROL ROOM

Bash led the group into a windowless white walled room. Inside were long folding tables, folding chairs, and laptops, wires, cords, and hard drives everywhere. Looking over the shoulder of a young blond Englishman was a tall and slender Asian. He stood around 6'1" and his black hair was cut like a City bankers. He wore a pair khaki trousers, brown leather boots, and a dark blue wool sweater. On his wrist was a smart watch of some kind on a rubber strap. The middle-aged Korean was youthful and handsome and flashed a white smile as the men entered. A dozen other young Asian men, a collection of glossy black hair and all clad in wool trousers, faded blue jeans, and wearing an array of wool and cashmere jumpers sat in front of glowing computers screens. The low murmur of Korean voices filled the room.

THE MERCHANT OF DEATH

'Good afternoon. Shall we begin the demonstration?' asked the tall South

Korean. This serene looking man was the CEO of a company that built combat drones, missile guidance systems, air-to-air missiles, and even torpedoes. He was an arms dealer. Definitely not the sort of gun runner the Revenant had encountered in the past. The tall South Korean belonged to a new generation of arms dealers.

The Merchant of Death smiled. 'The drones are now being controlled remotely by pilots back in Anyang. I am launching them from the ship now. They should arrive soon. Let's go outside.'

THE SNOWY FIELD
The Merchant of Death looked through a set of binoculars. In the distance were several derelict automobiles, trucks, and a T-55 tank. They had been towed out into the field. The Korean lowered the field glasses, turned, and smiled.

The Revenant, Jem, and the Texan stood next to their white UAZ. All three were looking through binoculars. Jem pushed a button on the binoculars and a digital screen appeared in his lenses and the focus intensified. Yes, it was a T-55 alright. The Texan and the Revenant both scanned the skies with their field glasses.

Bash and two young Korean men, both clad in dark blue parkas and faded blue jeans, stood next to the South Korean CEO's glossy blue Range Rover.

Suddenly a collection of sonic screams could be heard coming from the sky above. Through the clouds three dark shapes appeared—and then disappeared in a vortex of sound.

'Select a target,' asked the CEO to the group of men standing next to him.

'The black sedan,' replied the Revenant.

The CEO spoke into an encrypted smartphone—**a smartphone**—and ten seconds later the sedan exploded, the chassis being tossed into the air by the blast. A light grey and unmarked jet powered drone shrieked away and disappeared into the dark grey clouds above.

The Korean CEO smiled. 'That was easy. Now let me show you something new,' said the Merchant of Death.

The CEO then nodded in Bash's direction, and the South African, clad in white camouflage, started putting on a set of strange looking goggles and black gloves. (The gloves looked like something a scuba diver might wear). A moment later, the slim dark grey metallic googles were glowing with a bluish light in pulsating round patterns.

'Drones can be controlled from any point on the Earth. However, the equipment needed is bulky and requires a lot of space and a facility to house it. What my company has developed—with the financial support of Mr Holland—is the ability to control combat drones with wearable technology. Now pilots in the field can guide and direct the combat drones themselves whenever and wherever they like. No one in the world has technology this advanced,' said the Merchant of Death, and he laughed.

Bash walked forward; his eyes shrouded in luminous technology. The black gloves were covered in insulated wires. Bash barely looked human. He looked skyward; the goggles glowed with a new intensity; he brough up his hands, and like a conductor leading an orchestra, and he began.

A battleship grey combat drone broke through the clouds and then flew parallel to the field . Bash lifted his right hand and made a fist; the drone's jet engine glowed and the aircraft moved skyward. A few seconds later there was a loud explosion—a sonic boom—the combat drone was now moving at the speed of sound. The sound echoed off of the mountains like the hammer blows of an angry god.

'Select a target,' asked the CEO.

'The truck,' replied the Revenant.

Bash tilted his head one way and then another. A glowing point of light could be seen breaking through the clouds for an instant, and then the truck was blown apart; the cab of the large vehicle landing almost a hundred yards away from the rest of what remained of the truck. The vehicle was now nothing but unidentifiable burning wreckage. Pieces of it would continue to rain down from the sky for several more minutes after the initial explosion.

Bash pointed one of his gloved hands and suddenly the drone fly past them in a furious vortex of sound and shockwaves that could be easily felt by all present. The drone disappeared in the blink of eye behind one of the mountains.

The test had been impressive.

The Korean CEO smiled in a disarmingly innocent way. 'The drones are launched from a ship off the coast. They return between missions and can be quickly refueled and rearmed. I have ten more combat drones onboard the ship. One hundred more are en route from Korea now. They will arrive in three weeks. Transit will not be a problem. Everyone that has to be paid off, has been,' said the CEO in his mildly accented English.

Bash, with the glowing goggles tilted back on his head of white and grey hair, smiled. 'The ground forces will be fully protected by the drones. We can also easily shoot down any jet fighters sent against us. And we can control the drones from either South Korea or here. It's up to you. The remote control system is encrypted. The missile guidance systems are a cut above anything I have ever seen. Two dozen drone pilots are onboard the ship now. It looks like a regular cargo ship from the outside, but the facility below deck is fantastic. I've never seen anything like it,' said Bash.

It's amazing what billions of dollars can buy someone.

Three combat drones circled the skies above as they spoke.

'We will control the skies,' said Bash.

'Sounds good. When do move, General?' asked the Texan while looking at the Revenant.

'Soon.'

Gemma—The Carthage Option— Extraordinary Rendition

LONDON

The Spaniard looked at his dive watch: 7:53pm. The white hatchback idled in heavy traffic in a lightly falling snow. The driver just wanted to get home after a long day at the office. Traffic, that icy December night, was heavier than usual. There was a thin layer of snow on the ground. Christmas lights twinkled in store windows. Yes, half of London was Christmas shopping tonight, or so it seemed. The other half were just trying to get home.

And so, on a night in December, the driver of a white Volkswagen hatchback found himself pondering a problem: Who was following Enoch Tara's (supposedly) secret security unit? The driver was part of the unit that was being shadowed. The Special Unit's commander, who was also a former member of the Spanish Foreign Legión, had asked the retired legionnaire to look into it. The driver had, and he had come up empty. Both of these groups were elusive; however, in this case, the hunters had the advantage.

CABALLERO LEGIONARIO

The driver of the white hatchback had served in the Spanish Foreign Legión for twenty years. Retirement for the former NCO had lasted only six months. The small apartment in Ceuta had begun to feel like a coffin. The Brigada was only forty years old—still young. He had a daughter, but was legally separated from the mother, an Arab girl from the Spanish enclave of Melilla in Morocco. His wife was beautiful, as was their young daughter. Things hadn't worked out. His twenty-seven-year-old wife was living with his daughter in the apartment in Ceuta. He would wire money to her every month. Mr Tara paid extremely well. The apartment had been his free and clear; he had transferred ownership to his wife the day before he flew to London. He had bought his wife a new car—a white SEAT hatchback—just before he had announced that married life was not for him. His wife could not understand.

'Why are you divorcing me? Have I done something wrong?' she had asked through tears.

'No. It's my fault. I am not made for marriage. I'm neither a good husband nor a good father. Noor doesn't even like me.'

'That's not true. Your daughter loves you, as do I. Please don't leave me. I gave up my entire family for you,' she said, barely able to maintain her composure.

The Brigada, at the time, had remained unmoved. The whole marriage had been a mistake—for many reasons.

The Brigada was restless, and when one of his former commanders, a man who had risen through the ranks of Legión to become an officer, had emailed him from London and offered him a job, he accepted immediately. The job paid extremely well. The employer (Mr Tara) was generous; starting pay was £20,000 a month, plus employee benefits. Between the free housing in London (paid for by Enoch Tara), the free meals, medical insurance, a life insurance policy, expense advances, and the petrol allowance, one could live and work in London without even touching one's salary. And, most importantly, the retired NCO would have purpose again.

The Brigada's mother, a divorcée who had fled a violently abusive husband—the NCO's father—was furious with him when she found out. She loved her daughter-in-law, understood how much she had sacrificed to marry the legionnaire, and was shocked that her son could abandon his wife and daughter. How could he do this to his own family? Had his own mother's suffering meant nothing to him?

'I cleaned hotel rooms and scrubbed floors to support us. You promised me that if you ever married, you would never mistreat your wife,' his mother had shouted at him over the phone from her tiny flat in Madrid.

The Brigada had listened in silence. Everything his mother was saying was true. He was in the wrong, and he knew it. It was then that the reality of what he was doing had started to set in. He felt guilty. His wife, an Arab

Muslim, had had to leave Melilla for Ceuta. Her family had disowned her. The Brigada had told her that he loved her and promised to always stay with her.

'How can you do this?' asked the Spanish Legionnaire's mother.

He didn't have an answer.

A week after arriving in London, he found out that his mother, at his wife's request, had moved in with her and was helping to raise their daughter in Ceuta.

He sent his wife £3000 a month. He wired his mother £2000 a month. His mother accepted the money, but she was felt it nothing but a way for him to assuage his guilt. And, it was his obligation to take care of his family, whether he wanted one or not.

Every time he telephoned, his mother would berate him quietly and coldly. The Brigada had always pointedly refused to speak with his wife. The Brigada's mother would then carry the phone into his young daughter's room and hand her granddaughter her smartphone.

'Where are you?' his seven-year-old daughter had asked him over the phone the night before.

'I'm in London. How are you?'

'I'm sad. Mummy is sad. Everyone is sad,' she replied in in her usual mixture of Spanish and Arabic.

'Did you get the shoes I sent you?'

'Yes.'

'Do they fit?'

'Yes.'

'What would you like for Christmas this year?'

'Nothing.'

NORTH LONDON

Unbeknownst to the former legionnaire, his attempts to discover the
identities of the people following Tara's Special Unit had drawn attention to
himself. The Brigada had been discreet, really quite careful, but the group
that he was looking for was highly cunning and extremely dangerous.
Declan was on to him. The retired British Para now had photos and **a
name**.

The Spaniard was slender, athletic, and extremely handsome—good looking
in a uniquely Iberian way. And at the same time, he also looked
frighteningly brutal. **It was not the Legión that had made him tough**, it
was life that had done that. The Legión had simply honed his abilities.

The traffic slowed further as he approached his semi-detached. If he had
been riding in a friend's car or in the back of taxi, he would have gotten out
and walked home. He was that close.

Ten minutes later he turned off the main road and drove down a
cobblestone side street.

That's when the legionnaire realized he was being followed.

Alright: one dark blue (or was it black?) Audi A6 directly behind him. Yes,
it had been either directly behind him, two or three cars back, or off to the
side earlier that night. Yes, he had noticed. He wasn't sure what to make of
it; after all, perhaps they were driving home in the same direction? When he
turned off onto the narrow cobblestone side street, the Spaniard knew that
violence was in the offing. He remained calm.

He slowed just before his house—and then he gunned it. The small
hatchback surged forward; the Audi's headlights brightened; the Spaniard
was partially blinded and disoriented as the interior of his car filled with

bright light. The Legionnaire could only estimate his position on the street; the small hatchback had the advantage: it was small and much more maneuverable. **He took the risk** and drove forward; he turned sharply to the right—the car's interior went dark again; his eyes quickly readjusted and he moved forward down the street. The turn had been successful.

Behind him, the Audi was backing up and slowly turning; this gave the Spaniard the time he needed to escape. Both sides of the street were lined with parked cars, barren trees, street lamps, and all of it was under a thin layer of snow. Behind him he could see that the Audi had been joined by another car. Now two sets of headlights were following him down the cobblestone street at a high rate of speed.

The Spaniard turned onto another street and the Volkswagen accelerated. There wasn't any traffic on this partially illuminated street at all. He didn't bother looking in the rear view mirror; it didn't matter who was behind him. He had to escape. Without a doubt, more cars would soon appear and join the chase. He was outnumbered and outgunned. Escape was his only real option.

Declan's idea was to ambush and incapacitate the Spaniard with stun guns. He would then be tied up and quickly thrown into the trunk of one of the stolen cars his men were driving. They would take the Spaniard to an abandoned factory on the outskirts of London (there were a countless number of abandoned factories in this de-industrialized country) and interrogate him. Afterwards, they would dispose of the corpse. They needed to know the identities of Enoch Tara's hidden security unit. Carter Holland needed to know. Declan didn't know why (Declan was completely unaware of Carter's nation building plans)—Declan wasn't even curious. He had never even heard of Enoch Tara until a week ago. An Internet search had turned up little beyond the billionaire's official biography. All Declan knew was that this Spaniard was part of the Tara's secret security team, and he would, undoubtedly, have all the information Carter Holland needed.

Declan was driving a dark blue Audi A6 that a member of his younger brother's criminal gang had stolen in St John's Wood and delivered to Declan just an hour before. Next to him was another ex-Para. The Para in the front passenger seat was talking on a two-way radio. A myriad of voices and loud static filled the car's interior.

'Don't lose him! Yes…I can see him! Where is…Wait! Okay…Alright. Turn right! There he is! He's turned right!' It seemed like dozens of people all trying to talk at the same time intermixed with rivers of static.

'He's headed toward the church…He's just turned off.'

There was more static and then a minute later a voice shouted over the radio, 'We have him cornered!'

THE GERMAN

The tall and slender German had been born into a family of Prussian Junkers. His family had remained wealthy despite fighting on the losing side of two world wars. After completing his mandatory military service in the Bundeswehr, the young Prussian had joined the Spanish Foreign Legión in the final wave of foreign recruits allowed to enter before the new socialist government had banned any more intakes of foreign volunteers. The German had been restless. Life, even with money, had been a hollow one for him. The harshness of the Legión is what he had wanted and what he had found. He had also found in its ranks, comrades—no, brothers. Von was in the Spanish Foreign Legión for three years, and then he departed for the Croatian Army and the war in Croatia in 1991.

The young aristocrat, with a noble family name, had found himself being called the prefix 'Von' by his comrades in the Legión.

The Spaniard now cornered in a church yard was one of them.

¡A mí la Legión!

The Brigada had managed to telephone Von on his encrypted smartphone while evading his pursuers. The middle-aged, blond Prussian was running out the door of his house before the call had even ended. Von had telephoned their commander while en route to the church. The Comandante, a Legión comrade to both men, was on his way, and summoning others to join them.

THE SIDE STREET

Von found the white Volkswagen hatchback parked on a side street with its lights on and the driver's side door open. There were tire tracks and several sets of footprints up and down the narrow street. A thin layer of snow already covered the car. Von had avoided London traffic and had instead taken the Underground directly to the closest subway station. Von had run all the way to the church. In total, from the ringing of the phone until he had arrived at the church, had taken twenty minutes.

It was dark and still snowing when he spotted the car. The freezing cold weather had kept everyone indoors. Von, in faded blue jeans, a black leather jacket, and black Chelsea boots, moved through the darkness carefully looking and listening to everything around him. He drew his (unmarked) Yugoslav pistol. He stopped a few feet from the abandoned car; being careful to avoid the illumination the dome light and headlights gave off. He was in shadow. In the snow, he could make out several sets of footprints leading away from the car.

Von followed them through the darkness cautiously. With a drawn pistol.

THE CHURCH

The first thing that the Prussian noticed was the blood splattered on the walls, double doors, and snowy steps of the grey stone church. There were drag marks belonging to a body, bleeding heavily and most likely dead, which had been dragged away through the snow, to a waiting car where now only tire tracks remained.

The Spaniard had fought ferociously.

The large wooden double doors to the Medieval church were closed, Von cautiously opened one of them—a shaft of light flooded out. He looked into the church through the narrow gap in the door. Nothing beyond wooden pews, paned glass windows, and the grey stone slab floor.

And then he noticed the blood on the stone floor.

To hell with it. Von pushed open the door and rushed inside the stone church with his pistol drawn.

There was blood splattered and smeared down the center aisle of the church. There were also shell casings. A gun fight had taken place inside the church. The Medieval church was not brightly lit. Only a few wall mounted lamps had been left on for the few (if any) who came to pray, and perhaps, contemplate their lives. The church appeared to be empty. Had the dead body been the Spaniard's?

'Von,' said a choking voice near the stone altar.

Von rushed forward, slipping and almost falling down in the blood as he did so. He found the Spaniard mortally wounded and slumped up against the back of the stone altar. Blood was pouring out his wounds. The Brigada's face had been slashed open with a straight razor and he had suffered gunshot wounds to the chest, arm, and hand. An empty automatic pistol and shell cases lay at the Spaniard's side.

Von quickly took off his leather jacket and then his white dress shirt. He started to tear it into strips in order to bind his comrade's wounds.

'Von…Stop…I'm not going to make it.'

The German stopped, looked at the wounded Brigada, and then went down on one knee. Von cradled the Spaniard in his arms, blood was pooling around them. The Spaniard spoke while choking up blood.

'It was an abduction attempt. I shot four of them…I think. Von…Thank you. Now I don't have to die all alone.'

The Spaniard realized—too late—as his life ebbed away, how much he actually loved his wife and daughter. He missed them and now he knew that he would never see them, or his beloved and deeply disappointed mother, again. But it is always at one's lowest point, when there is only despair, that one can finally see things clearly.

Gemma—The Carthage Option—The Bright Young Thing

LONDON

Louise, in the dark wood coffered paneled offices of Occidental Prometheus Publishing Limited, felt overwhelmed. Yes, the publishers, though a small company, would pay her an advance of £3000 pounds and agreed to give her forty percent of the proceeds from the sales of her novel. Louise was thrilled. She couldn't believe it; she was about to become a published author.

The editors showed Louise copies of both the high-quality paperback and hardcover editions the company had already published. The editors also showed Louise a special folio edition they issued with their most popular books. Yes, if Louise novel sold well, they would issue a special folio edition of it. Really. Louise also discussed the art work she would like to have for the cover. The diminutive, strawberry blonde Louise in faded blue jeans, a heavy knit beige jumper, and her red, blue, and purple All Saints scarf, looked over past covers and the suggestions offered by the staff. Louise really didn't like any of them. This novel was hers; she wanted the cover to be hers too. The staff understood.

'Would it be possible to have the picture of an English country house on the cover?' asked Louise.

'Of course. Would you like a photo, drawing, or painting of one? asked the senior editor.

Louise, standing in the center of the office with her arms crossed thought about it for a for few minutes. This was an important decision. The cover had to be perfect.

The flaxen haired Aurelia, in faded blue jeans, a light grey cashmere sweater, and a blue quilted jacket, fascinated by what was happening, sat in the old leather armchair in the corner of the office, and drank it all in. Would this afternoon in the office become part of literary history? Was Aurelia witnessing history?

'I would like it to be a water color of a country house. Would that be possible?' asked Louise.

'Yes. We have some on file. Or we can have one painted for the cover. Do you have a particular house in mind?' asked the senior editor.

'Yes. One in the Lake District.'

6 THE WHITE STAG

Gemma—The Carthage Option—Jinx and Rex

THE MIDLANDS

The small forgotten town that surrounded Midlands-Hasegawa University had one cinema. The small, single screen theater, still referred to as a 'movie palace' by some, had been opened in 1923. Retired Army Major E. C. Tate OBE, born to English parents in British Ceylon, and the former owner of a large tea plantation in Sabaragamuwa, had built the cinema after selling the planation and moving to England.

The foyer's décor could best be described as 'British Raj Art Deco'. The theater (or rather amphitheater) itself could seat one hundred in blue velvet upholstered chairs, and its walls were decorated with white plaster Art Deco flourishes and innovative recessed lighting. The theater walls, covered by blue velvet drapes of cloth, gave way to a white ceiling punctured by almost a hundred small lights that, when the theater darkened, looked like a starry night sky. The silver screen was hidden behind a set of blue curtains. The cinemas original Art Deco Compton organ still stood in orchestral pit in front of the stage.

The local cinema, popular throughout the 1920s, 30s, and 40s, had struggled financially throughout the 1950s and been closed by the family in 1961. The small theater could no longer compete with the much larger modern cinemas that had popped up in the surrounding area.

The family turned the cinema into a venue and rented it out to various local organizations to host seminars, as a political campaign headquarters for the local MP, the occasional private film screening, local auctions, a regional theatre company, and the annual film festival that had once been held by Midlands-Hasegawa. All of that had come to an end in the late 1980s. The once ornate cinema had become too dilapidated to be rented out any longer. The grandchildren could no longer afford to properly maintain it, and so the family decided to shutter it completely in 1988.

Throughout the 1990s and the first decade of the new century, dozens of potential buyers had appeared. All of them had wanted to demolish the building and replace it with a large private home, a bank branch, a grocery store, or a block of flats. The family had always refused to sell. This small cinema was part of the family's heritage. They continued to hope that one day they would be able to restore it to its former grandeur and reopen it as a movie theater again.

In 2013, the family sold their house in London and decided to invest the money in the cinema. It took years to find the right contractors, architects, craftsmen, and plasters necessary to resurrect the structure and restore it. The situation at Midlands-Hasegawa had also changed. Hundreds of wealthy Asian undergraduates, many of them avid moviegoers, now attended the forgotten university in the small forgotten town in the Midlands.

THE ART DECO CINEMA
The cinema reopened in 2017 and was an immediate success. The undergraduates loved the Art Deco décor and enjoyed the convenience of being able to walk to a cinema just two blocks away from the main gates of the university. The cinema showed an unusual array of films, many of them Asian. All of the films were subtitled in English, even the English language ones (to make them more easily understood by the foreign undergraduates). Movies screened on Fridays at midnight were the most popular; movies featuring ghosts were shown and the theater was always sold out.

The real money, however, was to be found in the concession stand. The owners sold not only popcorn, but a huge selection of candy from across the world. Moviegoers had their choice of Japanese, Taiwanese, Korean, Swiss, German, American (and yes) British treats. The popcorn came in a variety of flavors too. Beyond the usual soft drinks, the cinema also installed an espresso machine and the Art Deco cinema became a de facto coffee shop. The once bankrupt cinema had become a cash cow.

The cinema also featured popular independent films. And, it was because of this, that Rex found himself sitting next to Jinx in a nearly empty theater on an icy Tuesday morning in mid-December. Yes, the first show on a weekday morning always had a small audience. Jinx had won a Best Actress award at a film festival in Tokyo (that she had not been able to attend because of the fashion show) for a film that she had acted in the summer before entering Muddy Hills. She wanted to see the film with Rex. There were only five others watching the film that morning. (All of whom recognized Jinx immediately after the show. All of them were students, and all of them smiled and nodded to her in acknowledgement.)

Jinx had returned from Mercia to discover that her award-winning film had opened at the local cinema on Saturday night to packed theaters. Jinx (or Jane as she was known to the Dons and administrative staff) was now not only the new 'It Girl' of Japan, but a movie star in England. Well, sort of. Jinx was still a relatively unknown actress in England, but there was no doubt that she was headed for stardom. Jinx's first lecture (Latin) that morning had seen the students clapping when she entered the lecture hall. Even the instructor happily congratulated her. Yes, the film was good, and Jinx's performance was extraordinary.

'I have never cried so much at the end of a movie, Jinx,' said Nara, a teenage Korean undergraduate, after class, in the hallway.

'Jinx, you are a natural, a fantastic actress. I can't wait to see you on stage in The Ptolemies,' said Hadley, an undergraduate, Hon, and aviatrix from Sussex.

Julie, an Asian undergraduate and a former classmate of Jinx at The Borders school in Wales, also congratulated her after class.

'Jinx, I knew when I watched you in the school play that one day you would be a movie star. I loved the film. It really captured your true nature. You are truly a great actress.'

'Oh, thank you, Julie,' replied an emotional Jinx.

Yes, Jinx had acted in the school play at The Borders every year.

Julie was an outgoing, sweet, and beautiful teenage undergraduate from South Korea. She had learned to speak Welsh and nearly flawless English while attending The Borders school in Wales with Jinx. Julie had been one of Jinx's first friends at the small girl's school. Julie's opinion really meant a lot to Jinx. Julie also often wore the dark blue (with a white strip down the middle) wool school scarf. Yes, Julie, like Jinx, was an Old Borderer.

As Jinx walked down the hallway towards her room in the residence hall, students would smile and tell her how much they liked the movie (albeit, one with a sad ending), and what a great actress she was. Jinx felt overwhelmed and very, very happy. Jinx couldn't believe her success. No, she really wasn't famous, and she certainly wasn't rich, the contract she signed with the swimwear company in Japan had netted her £200,000 pounds, half of which (at least) would be lost to tax. Still, she would have a small fortune left over, and there were doubtless more offers to come. Jinx felt suddenly dizzy as she made her way down the narrow hallway, the hardwood floor creaking under her with almost every step. Yes, Jinx had made it. At least it seemed so. And she was only eighteen.

THE INDEPENDENT FILM

The ninety-two minute film, a low budget costume drama set in England in 1901, saw Jinx, the young heroine, in a doomed relationship with a young subaltern. The film, though low budget, didn't look it. The film had been shot entirely on location in a small village in England and on a mountain in Wales, which substituted for the Indian frontier, and the costumes had all been made by talented interns. The young cinematographer, a recent film school graduate from Northern England, had used innovative techniques to produce beautiful scenes. The use of color and light made the young Jinx look even more beautiful.

Sometimes Rex would look over at Jinx in awe. Jinx was a true actress, and, he hoped, that she loved him as much as he loved her. (Of course, Jinx noticed his subtle glances, but pretended not to.)

One of the last scenes made Jinx cry. She hadn't expected to. She had rehearsed the scene with her young English co-star a hundred times, but their love on screen seemed so real that she could not help herself.

'It's not fair, Edward. It's not,' said Jinx, in a high collared white cotton dress (with a large white cotton collar) on the movie screen, tears streaming down her face. Jinx's long glossy black hair framed her face; the contrast between her pale complexion, blue eyes, and black hair was stark and beautiful.

The young couple were standing under a large leafy green tree in front of a dry stone wall. The couple were partially shaded by its branches; golden rays of sunlight broke through the leaves and danced on their heads and shoulders. The cinematography was inspired; the way the camera had been able to capture the sunlight, the contrast between the green leaves of the tree and the grey stone of the wall, and the actors in the scene was amazing.

'I never imagined that my parents would be so cruel. If I can't marry you, Jane, then I won't marry anyone,' replied the handsome young actor in a khaki uniform. The young actor then took Jinx's hand in his and said, 'I love you, Jane. I can't imagine life without you.'

Jinx, her pale blue eyes filling with tears replied, 'I love you, Edward. And because I love you, I don't want you to be alone. We can't marry, but there will be someone someday that you can, and I want you to marry her and be happy. Promise me that you will be happy one day.'

The young subaltern, blond and blue eyed, shook his head slowly, and said, 'No. I will wait for you. One day, my parents will no longer be an obstacle, and we will marry. I will wait for you, Jane.' And with that, the young man started to cry.

Rex was deeply moved by the scene too. Now it was Jinx stealing glances, and Rex's reactions made her happy. Rex was sweet and good hearted. Of course, he had found the scenes moving; of course he had.

The final scene of the movie showed the young khaki uniformed Edward in a rocky gorge surrounded by a squad of khaki clad British soldiers with Enfield rifles. The soldiers were shooting at a group of attacking tribesman somewhere on perilous northwest frontier of India, when suddenly, of all things, Edward is struck in the chest by an arrow and crumples to the ground dead.

Jinx and Rex were both crying quietly by the end.

The screen went black, the closing music of the soundtrack replaced the sounds of war, and the film credits began to roll. And there, on the silver screen, was Jinx's name. (Well, the film company used Jane, her legal name.)

Jinx was thrilled, finally, her name on the silver screen. Jinx still had tears in her eyes when she turned to Rex and asked, 'What do you think, Rex? Is it a good film?'

Rex smiled. 'It's a fantastic film. You are a great actress, Jinx, and I feel privileged to have been able to watch the film with you in a cinema.'

Rex spoke in such a sincere way that it left Jinx deeply moved. Yes, Rex was very sweet and kind. He was thoughtful. Rex was beautiful. And Jinx loved him.

'I'm happy that you liked the film.'

'Jinx.'

'Yes.'

'Would you like to have lunch with me in my rooms today? I'll bake you a potato in my fireplace.'

'Yes. I would like that.'

Gemma—The Carthage Option—The Pharaoh

LONDON
Carter Holland, shirtless, but wearing pale blue pyjama trousers, watched the television news report in silence. He had been shaving with a straight razor when something on the television drew his attention. Carter's face, still partially covered in white shaving cream and holding an open straight razor, had emerged from the white tiled bathroom a moment earlier. Now, he was staring at the large flat screen on the wall opposite him in rapt attention.

Declan had failed.

And more than that, Declan had drawn the attention of Scotland Yard and perhaps even MI5. And, most worryingly, and undoubtably, Declan's botched rendition attempt had drawn the attention of Enoch Tara and Tara's Special Unit.

THE SPECIAL UNIT
For the first time in Carter Holland's life, he was afraid. For the first time in Carter Holland's life, he had doubts. This one incident in an ancient and largely forgotten church in London had changed everything.

The Special Unit, a group of foreign mercenaries and intelligence operatives, was now looking for those responsible for their comrade's brutal murder. These were no ordinary men. Their mysterious Spanish commander didn't even have a name, and yet, Carter could already feel the Spaniard's breath on the back of his neck.

The Revenant would be back in a couple of days. The Revenant would know what to do. Yes, the mercenary warlord would know exactly what to do. Wouldn't he? The Revenant was far more dangerous than the Spaniard. Wasn't he? Couldn't the Revenant protect him from the wrath of the Special Unit? If the Spaniard found out that Carter had signed off on the abduction and killing of the Brigada, he would kill Carter for sure. It would be important to create a cordon sanitaire around himself. How many people, besides Declan, knew that Carter had authorized the abduction attempt against the Brigada?

Declan had botched it. How was that possible? How could a dozen men fail to capture one?

Why did he have to hear about this from a news broadcast? Why hadn't Declan contacted him immediately and told him himself? Where was he? Carter should not have had to learn of this fiasco from the BBC. Was Declan wounded in the foiled attacked and in hiding? Had Declan gone to ground? Was Declan dead? He had better be dead. It would be better for Carter if Declan were dead. Yes, that would be better. Dead men tell no tales. Yes, Declan's failure had been his undoing. Declan had sealed his own fate. Carter could not allow Declan to live. If Declan were taken alive, either by the police or Tara's Special Unit, then all of Carter Holland's plans would come to an ignominious end. Carter Holland would come to an end.

Carter Holland walked over to the one of the large paned glass windows on the fourth floor of his house in Mayfair. It was another overcast grey winter day in London. The city was an ocean of white filled with dark shapes.

Carter took a step back and his reflection appeared in the window. Carter's toned body, his well-defined abdominal muscles, his well-developed chest, and his muscular arms looked ghost like in the glass. **Discipline** had built up Carter's body. A strict diet, regular exercise, and harsh training had transformed him. It was **discipline** that had made Carter Holland a billionaire. It was **discipline** that had allowed Carter Holland's plans to reach this point—Carter was on the very cusp of creating a new country. **Discipline**. And it was **discipline** that would save him. Suddenly Carter felt a rush of energy surging through his body; his body seemed to grow stronger. No—Carter was now stronger than he had been just a moment ago.

Carter Holland's mind flooded with possibilities. No—this would not be the end of Carter's ambitious plans. No—this was not the end of Carter

Holland either. The Cosmos had not placed Carter Holland on the Earth to have him fail. Carter Holland would not end his existence on this planet as a failed demi-god. Carter Holland would succeed where others had failed. Carter Holland's name would echo to the far corners of the Universe. Carter Holland would, like Hercules, ascend into Heaven and become a god. Carter would be a God Emperor. That was Carter Holland's destiny. **Nothing would stand his way.** Nothing. Not even Enoch Tara and his elusive Special Unit.

Carter Holland looked at his reflection in the glass once more. His muscles were pulsing with energy. Carter, at 52, suddenly felt thirty years younger. Fear had vanished. Carter was now as fearless as he had ever been. Carter had been restored. The last few minutes had been a revelation. Carter was invincible. The Cosmos had set him on an unstoppable path. Carter had, from birth, been on an unstoppable trajectory. Carter had only to fulfill his destiny, and to do that he required one attribute more than any other:

Discipline.

Gemma—The Carthage Option—The Ptolemies

THE MIDLANDS

Rex's second floor white walled rooms in the residence hall were surprisingly warm. Midlands-Hasegawa's boilers were still out. The fireplace functioned well and the orange glow from the fireplace illuminated Jinx's smooth beautiful face. Rex's view of Jinx had changed—in some ways. To Rex, Jinx was still the sweet and good-hearted girl from Surrey. Jinx was beautiful. Jinx had always been beautiful. Jinx possessed **the quintessential beauty of an English girl**, a pale, ethereal and anxiously elegant beauty. The teenage Rex had loved her at first sight. They had connected at the first meeting of the Rhodesia Club. Both had already suffered tragedy, and both were doing their best to survive in an increasingly hostile world. The future was so uncertain now. Was there a future?

In other ways, Rex was in awe of the eighteen-year-old Jinx. She had found immediate success in film and the world of fashion. Rex wasn't jealous. He was happy for Jinx. Yes, like most everyone else at Muddy Hills, Rex couldn't help but view her in a different light. Rex couldn't believe that the unknown girl he had met last September was now on the brink of international stardom. Jinx hadn't changed at all. She was the same person she had always been. Fame hadn't affected her—not yet. Rex didn't think it ever would.

Rex only wanted to be happy. To have a modest life and find joy with those he loved would be enough. Rex knew that if he had Jinx at his side, then the harshness of the world would be bearable. Without Jinx, it would not.

However, Rex had a secret. He was fragile. His heart was not strong. The same aliment that had ended his father's life, had afflicted his. Rex had no idea how long he would live. The doctors couldn't answer that question. When, one day, Rex passed away and joined his father on the other side, Jinx would be left alone, as would Rex's mother. It wasn't fair to marry Jinx only to possibly leave her so soon. It would be the height of selfishness.

Rex looked at his reflection in the mirror over the mantelpiece. He was alive. He was breathing; his heart was beating. Yes, Rex's fragile heart was still beating. Life. Rex found himself momentarily lost in thought. Yes, life. The fragile, fleeting, and transient quality of life itself. Life: God's most precious gift. And God's most unappreciated one. Rex appreciated his life more than most; more than anyone he knew—except for his mother. Rex's Rhodesian mother loved him and she knew that he would not have a full life. It grieved her; it wounded her. Eventually, it would destroy her. When Rex died, she would be all alone in the world. Rex felt a wave of deep sadness welling up in him. It wasn't fair. It wasn't. Rex would live his life to the fullest. He would love and be loved, for as long as he could. However, was it fair to Jinx? No, it wasn't fair at all.

The eighteen-year-old fresh faced Rex looked away from the mirror. Rex, in dark khaki trousers, a white button-down Oxford dress shirt, and white slippers walked over to the fireplace and looked at Jinx. He smiled. The beautiful, slender, elegant, and kind Jinx was poking at a baked potato Rex had baked for her in the fire place.

'Can I help you with that?' asked Rex gently.

Jinx, her pale face framed by her glossy, jet-black chin length bob, smiled.

'Yes, please, Rex. Another fork, please.'

'Oh, yes, to answer your earlier question, my co-star kept calling me by my real name, Jane, instead of the character's name, which was Isabelle. After three days of shooting, and repeated takes, the director finally decided to change the name of character,' said Jinx laughingly.

Rex walked over to the wooden table next to the window and retrieved a metal fork. He then sat down across from Jinx in one of the wooden chairs in front of the fireplace. He handed her the fork. Jinx, in denim blue jeans and a white blouse, took it and used both of her forks to tear open the potato on the white ceramic plate in her lap.

'Thank you, Rex. This is just what I needed.'

Jinx then noticed the forlorn expression on Rex's face. She froze.

'What's wrong, Rex?'

The blond, slender, good hearted, and beautiful Rex sighed.

'What's wrong, Rex? Please tell me.'

'I love you, Jinx. All I want to do is spend the rest of my life with you.'

Tears welled up in Jinx's eyes. These were the words she had wanted to hear from Rex from the moment she had met him, and now, on a cold wintery afternoon, he was saying just that. Jinx stood up and put the plate with the steaming baked potato on the table. She walked over to Rex. Rex rose to meet her. She hugged him tightly and said, 'I love you, too, Rex. I promise I will always be with you. I need you, Rex.' Jinx was crying softly as she spoke.

Rex, tears forming in his eyes, broke from the embrace and said, 'I have something to tell you, Jinx. Please sit down.'

'What's wrong, Rex? Whatever it is, we will face it together.'

'Jinx, I have a heart condition. The same condition that killed my father. I can't promise you a long life together. I love you, Jinx; and because I love you, I want you to know how uncertain our future will be if you stay with me,' said Rex quietly.

Jinx felt a shudder go through her as Rex spoke. Poor Rex. Poor sweet Rex. It's wasn't fair. Why had God blessed her with Rex only to deny him a healthy heart? It wasn't fair. Why must Jinx and the ones she loves suffer so much? And, at that moment, **Jinx felt blessed.** In spite of everything that had happened to her, and to Rex, they had been blessed to find each other.

'Even if our lives together are brief, I want to spend as much of it as possible with you. Every precious moment of it, Rex,' said Jinx through tears. 'I love you, Rex. I will be at your side for as long as God allows. Life is so fleeting. One is blessed to have even a few brief moments happiness. Whenever I am with you, I am happy, Rex.'

THE SNOWY FIELDS OF MUDDY HILLS

Rex, in faded blue jeans and a dark blue parka, walked along side Jinx through the snow. While still cold, the fiery sun now radiated through small breaks in the clouds. Rays of golden light broke through and illuminated the buildings and fields around them. Jinx, clad in a dark grey wool jacket, denim blue jeans, and her Blue and white Borders scarf, smiled.

'I love snow. It's beautiful,' said Jinx happily through chattering teeth.

'Yes, so do I,' replied Rex, and he smiled. Jinx loved him as much as he loved her. Now there were no doubts. Rex was the happiest he had ever been. The future, so uncertain, and even frightening, was suddenly brighter.

The couple walked towards the large Portland stone Rhodes theatre together. When they reached the steps of the large stone structure, Rex extended his hand to Jinx; Jinx grasped it. The warmth moved through both of them. Jinx smiled.

'Let's walk up the steps together,' said Rex, his breath materializing around him in the freezing cold air. Rex was beautiful. And more importantly—yes, more importantly, he was kind and good-hearted. It was not looks alone that had attracted Jinx to Rex. It was his kind soul. As Jinx ascended the stone staircase, she felt herself becoming lighter. Rex's words had freed her in a way she had not expected. Jinx had found love. And love had freed her. God had not abandoned Jinx. Nor had He abandoned Rex. Jinx was filled with hope.

Half way up the stone steps, Rex noticed something. 'Look!' said Rex excitedly as he pointed in the direction of the snowy field beyond the school grounds.

Jinx turned and looked out across the field. And there it was: a white stag. It was actually white. The powerfully built creature had an otherworldly quality about it.

'A white stag, Jinx!' said Rex happily. 'They are one in 30,000. One is blessed to see even one in their life time. It means something.'

Jinx, still focused on the majestic white stag which was serenely making its way through the snow choked field asked, 'What do you think it means, Rex?' Jinx knew of the myths surrounding the White Stag; she was curious to know what the White Stag meant to Rex.

'It is a harbinger of some monumental event to come.'

'What do you think it will be?' asked Jinx.

' I don't know,' said Rex quietly as he slowly turned his head from side to side. 'But, I know, whatever happens, happens for a reason.'

Jinx and Rex watched the white stag cross the snow white field slowly until it disappeared back into the forest. Rex grew reflective in those final moments. Yes, the White Stag symbolized many things, not all of them good. Yes, something was about to happen which would change everyone's lives forever. And then Rex felt a wave of fear brush lightly over him. Rex looked out onto the snowy field for a moment more, oblivious to the cold.

'God's Will be done,' said Rex quietly.

Jinx also knew what the White Stag could portend. Yes, Rex and Jinx were both as English as they were Rhodesian. They knew.

'Come on, Rex, or we are going to be late for rehearsal,' said Jinx through chattering teeth. Jinx then extended her soft hand towards Rex and he grasped it. Whatever happened, they would have each other.

No, neither had taken out their smartphones and filmed it. No, that would have spoiled the magic. Somethings are meant to be witnessed, not merely photographed and downloaded. The white stag now had an even more powerful meaning to Jinx that it had before. They had seen it together. That alone made it special. What the white stag presaged that afternoon remained a mystery to her. However, soon, she would find out exactly what the white stag was heralding.

Gemma—The Carthage Option—The Comandante

MARBLE ARCH
It was the text message on Enoch's *other* encrypted smartphone that had alerted him to the potential danger. This particular cell phone was only used to communicate with the leader of Enoch Tara's Special Unit.

We must meet tonight. 7PM.

SURREY
The small stone Edwardian cottage, on three acres of heavily forested land, was owned by Enoch Tara through a series of off shore companies; not to avoid taxation, but detection. Whenever Enoch needed to meet with his secretive security team or a safe house to hide in, he would come here.

The three-bedroom house was lightly furnished. There were two or three single beds in each room. White cotton bedding, still in plastic, sat in cardboard boxes next to folded wool blankets on each bed. The main room had a few pieces of inexpensive furniture. The white walls were undecorated. Each room also had a single nightstand and a standing lamp.

Enoch had arrived at the house in a glossy dark blue Range Rover, its headlights cutting through the darkness as it entered the snowy woods surrounding the cottage, followed a few minutes later by two Audi A7s (one dark blue, the other polar silver). The six-member security team was ordered to remain outside and patrol the grounds.

Enoch, wearing a dark grey suit, pale blue dress shirt, and grey tartan necktie, shivered as he walked alone through the snow-covered grounds and trees towards the house, the snow crunching underfoot. As requested by the leader of the Special Unit, the men following Enoch in the two cars were (though illegal in England) armed with 9mm pistols. The situation had changed.

THE COMANDANTE

The Spaniard, born and raised in the Spanish enclave of Ceuta, had entered the Spanish Foreign Legión at eighteen. He was of average height, slender, but muscular. He had done what few privates in the Legión had done: He had become an army officer. The Spaniard spent twenty-two years in the ranks. The highly decorated and multilingual Comandante (Major) had retired at forty. However, bored at home alone in Ceuta, he looked for work of a very special nature. It was this desire for action that had led him to Enoch Tara. And now, here in a small cottage in Surrey, he had come to speak with his employer.

The Spanish Legionnaire who stood before Enoch had light brown hair (with a few silver hairs) and blue eyes. And at forty five, he was still physically fit and handsome. He wore a black suit, white shirt, and black tie. He was also armed (illegally) with a 9mm pistol. But then again, he was always armed. The Spaniard was not a lively man; he was quiet and reserved, not easily excited. He was brave and loyal—to his men and his employer— and in that order. He had worked for Tara for three years. He had never met any of Enoch's regular security detail. That was by design.

The Comandante (Major) had been pacing around the room when Enoch arrived out front. When Enoch entered the main room of the house, he was standing motionlessly next to the inexpensive armchair next to the entrance to the hallway.

'Thank you for coming, Mr Tara,' said the Comandante in flawless English.

'What has happened?'

'Mr Tara, I need a free hand.'

'You have always had a free hand.'

'I need a free hand.'

Enoch felt a slight shock move through him. Yes, he knew that if the head of his Special Unit ever contacted him, it was important. Now he realized that something terrible had happened.

'What's going on?' asked Enoch.

'In order to give you plausible deniability, I can't tell you,' replied the Comandante.

'I want to know. Give me some idea what has happened.'

'One of my men has been murdered. I have no doubts that the people responsible for it are the same ones who followed us to Corbridge.'

Enoch felt another, much greater shock, move through him. Enoch went white as a ghost.

'Murdered?' asked a clearly shocked Enoch.

'I need a free hand, Mr Tara,' asked the Comandante quietly.

Enoch felt as if someone had knocked the wind out of him. One of his men had been murdered. A man's life had ended—because of who he had been working for. Enoch felt his chest tighten. A deep feeling of grief and sorrow rose up inside him. Someone had been killed, albeit indirectly, protecting him. *A man had died protecting him.* Enoch suddenly felt light headed. Control yourself, Enoch. Now is not the time to lose your balance. **Focus**.

'Do you have any idea who is behind all of this? asked Enoch.

'No. None at all. Not yet,' replied the Spaniard.

Enoch stared at the Comandante for a moment. The svelte figure of the former Spanish Legionnaire stood ramrod straight before him. The Spaniard's chiseled face was like stone. The Comandante knew what he was doing. And, undoubtably, he had assessed the situation they now faced correctly.

After a moment more of reflection, Enoch's gazed into the Comandante's cold blue eyes and said, 'Alright.'

7 BRIGHTNESS FALLS

Gemma—The Carthage Option—Enoch and Gemma

LONDON
Gemma, in faded blue jeans and a white cotton blouse (with a large collar), had been making dinner in her studio flat when the intercom system activated. Gemma looked at her silver Cartier watch: 6:35pm. She walked across the room and looked at the small screen. It was Enoch and three of his security team. The svelte Enoch, at 5'9", looked tiny in comparison to the tall hard men standing on either side of him. It was the forlorn expression on his face that alarmed Gemma.

'Come up.'

The entrance door clicked and one of Enoch's men pushed open the door and entered the building first, followed by Enoch, and then the other two bodyguards.

Was something wrong?

THE APARTMENT
Gemma opened the metal door and invited Enoch to enter. Enoch, in a pair of dark khaki trousers, a white button-down Oxford dress shirt, and a dark blue cashmere overcoat, entered the small apartment.

The two security men waited outside in the hallway. That was different.

'Please have a seat at the table, Enoch. I've made mushroom soup and salad for dinner.'

'Thank you, Gem,' said Enoch quietly.

Gemma helped Enoch take off his overcoat. She noticed that he was wearing the same set of clothes, right down to the brown leather Oxfords, that he had purchased with her in Oxford on that pivotal trip last summer. Gemma hung his coat up on the coat rack next to the front door of her apartment.

Enoch ate little and said even less at dinner. Gemma was worried, but limited her conversation to the weather (she loved snow) and asking Enoch if wanted any more salad or soup; he didn't. At first, Gemma had felt that Enoch was just tired, but twenty awkward and nearly silent minutes into dinner, she wondered if something more was weighing on Enoch's mind.

'Are you ok?' asked Gemma gently, softly, quietly.

Enoch looked up at Gemma. His gentle demeanor wavered and the handsome, youthful face went pale. Enoch put his face into his hands and started to cry. Gemma felt her heart breaking. If Enoch was upset, then Gemma was too.

'I love you, Enoch. Whatever it is, we will face it together, alright?'

Enoch continued to sob quietly. Something terrible had happened. But what? Gemma stood up and walked around the table. She gently placed her hand on Enoch's shoulder and brushed it gently with her small soft manicured hand.

Enoch looked up at Gemma; he had tears running down his face; his lips were trembling. What could have happened to put Enoch in such a state?

Enoch spoke through tears and sobs, 'All I ever wanted to be was an actor,

Gemmy. I wanted you at my side. We could have been happy with a modest life. I never wanted any of this. I wish I could go back and have stayed an actor. Then none of this would be happened.'

'What's happened, Enoch?' asked Gemma quietly.

Enoch hesitated. Should he tell her? No. It would mean disclosing company information. He couldn't. Gemma worked for Millennium Investments. And he didn't want her to be frightened. Enoch was the target, not Gemma. No, he wouldn't burden her with the death of the Brigada. That a man with a wife and young daughter had been murdered by an unknown enemy in pursuit of information about Enoch weighed enormously on him. Enoch felt a deep sense of guilt and responsibility for the death of the Spaniard in the Medieval church. Yes, Enoch had read the After Action Report (AAR) from the Special Unit and the stories in the press. The Brigada had died a terrible death. He had suffered horribly. And Enoch could not escape that it had all transpired because an unknown enemy had wanted information about him. Enoch was being crushed under a wave of grief.

'Please tell me what is wrong, Enoch. I am here for you.'

'I love you, Gemma.'

'I love you, Enoch.'

Gemma now had tears welling up in her eyes. Enoch was a gentle soul, and she loved him for it.

'Enoch, let's just runaway. We can live in the Lake District in my country house.'

'That's no longer possible, Gem,' replied Enoch quietly. Enoch stared straight ahead. He was trembling.

'I wish I could just go back in time, Gemma. I want to be young again. I want to pick blackberries along the River Wey with my mother in the summer. I want to play cricket with my friends on the village green. I want to see my father again and hear him tell me how proud he is of my performance in the school play. I want to see the look on my parents' faces when I tell them that I have been accepted into Harrow. They were so happy. I was happy, Gemma. Life was so simple when I was young. Glorious summers, the scent of fresh apples, cobblestone streets, the smell of woodsmoke, daffodils, and being surrounded by endless fields of green. Putting on my school blazer for the first time. Talking with mother about…everything. I just want to go back, Gemma. And next time, Gemma, **I promise** that I won't run away from the theatre after the final act. After the play, I will find you backstage, and I will tell you how much I love you. I will tell you, Gemma,' said Enoch while choking back tears.

'And next time, Enoch, **I promise**, I will listen,' replied Gemma gently.

Gemma—The Carthage Option—CCTV

LONDON
The Comandante had the resources that only a multibillionaire like Enoch Tara could provide. Yes, the resources at the Spaniard's disposal were, for all intents and purposes, infinite.

The media reports regarding the Brigada's death were lurid and disturbing. And completely off the mark, as the modern mainstream media now usually is. No, the Brigada was not a gangster. No, the gunfight in the 12th century Medieval church was not part of an ongoing gangland war in London. No, there were no large amounts of cash or any drugs were found in the Brigada's semi-detached. No, the Brigada had not joined the Spanish Foreign Legión to avoid prison. No. No. No.

Only the Daily Telegraph had the story right; and by that, it had simply reported that Scotland Yard had no idea what had actually transpired in the church beyond a gun battle and that one man, reportedly a real estate developer, had been found dead at the scene. The police had spent two days gathering forensic evidence. The investigation was ongoing.

What the police had managed to keep out of the papers was that there was no CCTV in the area surrounding the sparsely attended Medieval church. The church, like many Anglican churches in London, was usually empty, even on Sundays. Post-Christian Europe had little need for God. At least, that is how many in Europe now felt. A local volunteer unlocked the church in the morning and he would return to lock it at 10pm. It was the church warden that discovered the Brigada's body and telephoned the police.

The Comandante and eight other members of the Special Unit had arrived a few minutes after the Brigada had died. The Comandante ordered that everyone leave the church immediately and meet at the safe house in Central London. The Brigada was to be left in the church. There was nothing else that could be done for him. The men understood. If they were dragged into the police investigation that followed, the Special Unit would be revealed and the unit disbanded. The mission was paramount. The mission: protect their employer.

While enroute to the church minutes earlier, the Comandante had alerted Enoch Tara's personal security team to make sure Mr Tara was secure in his Marble Arch panic room for the next few hours until the nature of the current threat could be determined. Enoch, having just finished dinner, followed his security chief's orders and retreated into the armored room for the next few hours. The security chief in Marble Arch could not say what was happening, only that the order had come in from the Special Unit.

This was not the first time Enoch had been retreated into the panic room. He always listened to the security chiefs. They could only protect Enoch if he listened to them. Enoch had spent the night in a narrow camp bed. The next morning, the text from the Comandante appeared on his smartphone.

Twelve members of the Special Unit had met at the semi-detached an hour after the Brigada had been killed. Von relayed what little information he had. Which was very little. The Comandante sent everyone home at midnight. The Comandante knew what was he was going to do—as soon as he discovered who had been behind the brutal death of his comrade. But he needed additional resources.

CCTV

London is easily one of the most surveilled cities in the world. CCTV cameras adorn virtually every street—except for the places you really need them. The Comandante had, because of Enoch's money and connections, full access to London's CCTV systems—virtually all of them—there wasn't just one. The Spaniard had used them in the past and he was using them again.

It was late. The Comandante's face was illuminated by the glow of the computer display in front of him as he glided his eyes across the screen.

Click.

With each click of the mouse, the camera position changed; a video replay slowed; an image was magnified. Sometimes the Spaniard would lean back in the wooden chair and stare out the second storey window of his house. It was snowing. The barren branches of the tall trees which lined the street in front of his house cast shadows into the room. The Comandante, in pale blue cotton pyjama trousers, white slippers, and a white t-shirt, was near collapse. Emotionally drained, and relying on black coffee to stay awake, the Comandante kept searching. Sometimes he would nod off and awake with a jolt. Keep searching. The information you need is here—somewhere.

The Comandante's mind was filled with flashes from the past. He had known the Brigada for over two decades. They had been comrades, true friends. Yes, the Brigada was a soldier; the possibility of a violent death came with the job. However, as much as the Comandante told himself that, he still couldn't escape the fact that if he hadn't offered the Brigada the job in the first place, this wouldn't have happened. No. The Brigada would not begrudge him for any of this. No. Stop torturing yourself. Perhaps the Comandante should have sent someone else to look for the elusive enemy? For some reason, the Comandante was convinced that the group in pursuit of the Special Unit was made up largely of foreigners. He didn't have any facts to support this, only a strong feeling. And his instincts usually turned out to be correct. The Brigada had the necessary interpersonal skills needed to find the information they were looking for. Yes, the Brigada's death had always been a possibility. The danger had been real. Both men had known that.

The Comandante was alone in his semi-detached house in Convent Garden. He had never married. With the exception of his childhood and the barracks in the army, he had always lived alone. He needed peace and quiet.

The Comandante had been able to locate some of the CCTV video of the Brigada's white hatchback and watch CCTV camera footage of parts of the pursuit through London—parts of it. Now he was trying to go backwards and trace the cars to their source. It hadn't been easy.

After two days of searching through hundreds of hours of CCTV footage, the exhausted Comandante found something.

Click.

What's this? The Comandante leaned forward and scanned the image before him. He magnified it. He paused and looked closely at the two men emerging from a dark alley between an empty store front and an office building. Both wore dark hoodies (drawn tightly around their faces), faded blue jeans, and thick black framed eye glasses. It was difficult to make out their faces.

A silver 2018 BMW M5 pulled up and a skinny driver (most likely a teenager) in a pair of blue jeans, trainers, and a hoodie, got out of the driver's side door. One of the two taller men got in on the passenger side of the car while the other walked around the front and opened the driver's side door. He climbed in and closed the car door. The teenage driver sprinted down the alley and disappeared into the darkness.

Then the driver made a critical mistake: He loosened his hood, took off his thick frame glasses, and unbeknownst to him, stared directly into a camera that had been placed above a door to a store across the street from where the silver BMW was idling.

Click.

Alright, he had an image. Now, let the facial recognition software do the work. A series of images flashed across the screen: the computer program was rapidly collating material and searching online data bases, including the criminal records at Scotland Yard and Interpol. With a final flash, the search came to an end.

And then, like a bolt of lightning, a name and face appeared on the computer screen.

Gemma—The Carthage Option—Constantinople

ISTANBUL

The eclectic city that unfolded before the Revenant was ancient. And modern. And like every winter in the Dardanelles, freezing cold. It was snowing; the Imperial city was blanketed in a white layer of snow, and more was continuing to fall. The Revenant made his way down the grey stone steps—ancient steps that Emperors had once descended. The sounds of voices echoed off of the high walls of the narrow, twisting alleyway.

Surrounding the Revenant were the Galata Tower, ancient aqueducts, and beneath his feet, an earthquake proof water storage system of cisterns; an engineering marvel which had been initiated by the Roman Emperor Hadrian in the 2nd century AD which had been continually expanded by Byzantine stonemasons for over a millennium.

The Revenant had not returned to England with the others. The Revenant had had to meet someone in Istanbul. The important meeting now over, the reluctant warlord was making his way back to his hotel in Pera. He would pack and fly back to London that evening.

Yes, soon, very soon, the war would begin. Victory would quickly follow. And soon after that, the Revenant would lead the Core Army and thousands of other volunteers to his ancestral homeland and free it once and for all. The Revenant, after decades of exile, would return. He would pray at the unmarked graves of his mother, wife and young daughter. He would apologize to them for failing to protect them. He would rebuild the house that had been destroyed by the evil beings that had destroyed his homeland. And he would seek revenge against those responsible for it all.

THE GOLDEN HORN

The recently renovated old hotel, of innovative interior design, which had been built on the foundations of an ancient Byzantine structure, was located at the end of a narrow alleyway, and now housed a (relatively) moderately priced twenty-three room hotel.

The Revenant had rented a room overlooking the Bosphorus. The hotel was owned by a German hotelier of Turkish origin. The minimalist décor of the hotel rooms appealed to the Revenant; the white walls were like clean slates. The beds were extremely comfortable, and the Turkish hotel staff, like all Turks, was polite and welcoming.

The hotel was also rarely, if ever, mentioned in travel guides. It offered a degree of privacy that few hotels in the city did. One could hide out here, if necessary. Most of the hotel guests were Germans or Germans of Turkish origin.

The Revenant, in a dark blue wool overcoat (with a fur collar), a black suit, white shirt, and black tie, passed through the large double doors of the hotel and walked through the lobby on his way to the front desk. He stopped and gazed out of one of the large windows which looked out onto the churning waters of the Bosphorus.

The Revenant wanted to find peace. He hadn't felt normal, calm, or at peace in decades. He wished he could go back and change things, but he knew he couldn't. Would vengeance bring him peace? No. It wouldn't, but it would provide him some solace. Why should the guilty continue to live? Why had God allowed them to live after all that they had done? When would they suffer? **And then an answer:** The Revenant was the instrument God would use to right the wrongs of this small corner of the world. Yes, it was all on his shoulders now. This heavy burden was just one more burden on the Revenant's shoulders. He had carried such a heavy burden on his shoulders for so long that the additional weight had barely been noticed. Now it had been.

God grant me peace.

The Revenant took the hotel key from the attractive young Turkish woman at the front desk. The young woman had honey blonde hair the color of Anatolian wheat; the same color hair that his wife and daughter had had. Yes, had his daughter lived, she would have been about the young Turkish woman's age.

'Sir, you have a parcel from London. It arrived just a few minutes ago,' said the desk clerk in her flawless English. She smiled and gave the Revenant the slender, thin cardboard envelope covered with airfreight stickers and a plastic envelope containing the customs declaration.

'Thank you.'

Jem had mailed him something via airmail from London. What could it be? The Revenant entered the café adjoining the hotel lobby and was seated by a white jacketed member of the staff.

'Yes, coffee, please.'

The war refugee, the exile, the soldier, tore the seal open on the parcel and took out the newspaper clippings from inside. Jem had cut them out from different newspapers and mailed them to the warlord.

The Revenant immediately noticed the headlines, the photos of the Medieval church, and of the murdered former member of the Spanish Foreign Legión. The warlord's blood ran cold as he read through news article after news article. The Revenant had no doubt that Carter Holland had ordered it. Carter Holland, left alone in London while the Revenant had overseen preparations abroad, had taken matters into his own hands. The impatient Carter Holland was becoming reckless after decades of careful preparation. They were so close to achieving their goals, and now Carter Holland was endangering it all. And for what? Was his hatred of Enoch Tara so deep that it was worth jeopardizing everything?

'Sir, your coffee,' said the young dark-haired woman as she smiled and placed the white porcelain cup and saucer on the marble table top.

'Thank you.'

The Revenant's cold blue eyes looked out across the icy waters of the Bosphorus. He knew that the London that awaited him was now on a war footing. A secret war was now being waged in England by secret armies. Enoch Tara's Special Unit would seek revenge. The still mysterious Spaniard, who's name the Revenant had yet to ascertain, would be waiting for him. Now, it was a race against time. A race to find out the identity of the Spanish commander of the Special Unit and eliminate him and his men; a race to begin the civil war in an all but forgotten country in Eastern Europe and secure victory and a create new country before the international community could react, and a race to return home and avenge his countryman and family before he was too old and frail to do so. The Revenant was so close, so close.

Gemma—The Carthage Option—The River

EAST ANGLIA
It was an extremely cold and overcast day in a snowy East Anglia. The vast snow-clad fields unfurled in every direction. Not a single manmade structure could be seen.

Louise was all alone. Louise, in faded blue jeans, a heavy beige wool jumper, and her blue, red, and purple All Saints scarf, walked through the small grove of leafless trees that lined the river. The diminutive and strawberry blonde Louise shivered against the cold. Louise felt calm. The cold was invigorating. And most importantly, Louise was home in East Anglia.

A single snow flake swirled in the wind before her, and then a few more appeared. Louise continued to walk down the river's edge as the snow began to fall. Ahead, an ancient stone bridge suddenly appeared. Louise had never seen it before. Louise pivoted and started to walk towards it. The snow began to fall lightly as she approached the bridge.

The ancient grey stone bridge looked to be thousands of years old. Was it Saxon? Roman? Louise couldn't tell. Louise walked to one end of the bridge and stared down the length of it. The other side of the snow shrouded river beckoned. Louise stepped onto the stone bridge and started to walk across it. Half way across, she stopped and walked to the low stone wall and leaned against it.

The clouds above were dark grey, light grey, and black, with wisps of white swirling within the churning overcast sky. It was a splash in the water that drew Louise's attention to the waterway below.

The river was shallow and smooth rocks appeared above the swirling waters below the bridge. Louise smiled. Yes, she was home. This land was Louise's ancestral home. Her ancestors had lived here for thousands of years. This soil was part of her, and when she passed away, she would return to it.

Another splash. Louise looked at the river below. And then she saw it.

The stream seemed to shift and move and then under the shallow eddies and ripples of the river, a large, dark, bat like wing appeared with a clawed hand. Then the black scales of a dragon appeared. The large dragon took shape suddenly and raised its glossy black head out of the water. Its inky black eyes stared at Louise. Louise froze. She was terrified. The dragon loomed up before the tiny little Louise. Its large black wings unfolded and cast a shadow through the gloom which blocked out and darkened the sky above her. Louise could hear the dragon breathing, slowly, steadily, and without the slightest trace of fear.

It was Louise that was afraid.

The spectral dragon turned its head to look northwest for a moment, and then it looked back at Louise. The dragon's pupilless black eyes captured Louise's gaze completely. She was unable to move. Louise trembled.

What did it want?

The supernatural creature swayed gently back and forth before her. Its large mouth opened slightly; Louise could see its long, sharp, white teeth just three feet away from her. She could feel its cold breath.

What did it want?

Tears streaked down Louise's face. Her lips trembled. She had to know. She had to ask it the question. She had to will herself to speak. Finally, her tiny body shaking, Louise asked, **'What do you want?'**

The dragon replied in an unintelligible whisper.

LONDON

Louise awoke with a jolt. It was dark. The street lamps outside the windows cast shadows across the white walls of the small room. She was in the lower bunk of the bed in the girls' residence hall at her university in London, far away from East Anglia. Her face was wet from tears. She had been crying in her sleep. She was breathing hard, almost gasping for breath. She looked around the room. Nothing. It was quiet. Louise was afraid. Was the dragon here, lying in wait?

Louise, in a pair of white and light blue paisley pyjama bottoms and a white t-shirt, slowly climbed out of bed. She stood up and looked around the room. She put on her white wool slippers and walked towards the windows. She looked down onto the paved street below. No traffic. Only lightly falling snow. What time was it? She looked at the glowing blue Arabic numerals on the digital clock: 3:32am.

She was trembling. This was no ordinary dream. Louise could sense that. Someone was in danger. But who? And from whom? Louise had no idea. Louise's mind seemed to go blank for a moment. And then it opened up and thoughts began to swirl around in her mind. And then Louie's mind went blank again. And then it opened with a violent jolt.

It was Aurelia who found Louise unconscious on the hardwood floor of their room the next morning.

Made in the USA
Middletown, DE
28 February 2022

61919806R00139